REAL
PEOPLE,
REAL LIFE,
REAL
GRACE

IT'S A
GOD
THING

STORIES TO HELP YOU EXPERIENCE

THE HEART OF GOD

WORTHY
Inspired

TABLE OF CONTENTS

PART 1

GOD'S
COMFORT

1

WILL I LOSE MY SON?

MARY DODGE ALLEN

I sat in the darkened room in Parkland Hospital's burn unit and listened in anguish as my four-year-old son whimpered in pain while he dozed, even though a constant dose of morphine dripped through his IV line. My mind, tormented by guilt, couldn't stop visualizing the agonizing moments three days earlier, when my carelessness had caused his painful burns.

It was dinnertime. Davey was sitting on his booster seat at the kitchen table. He had just had a bath and was dressed in lightweight pajamas. I opened the oven door and took out a glass baking dish. Its hot contents briefly fogged my glasses, and I realized too late that cheese sauce had bubbled over the sides, making the handles slippery. As I carried the glass dish to the table, I tried to maintain my grip, but my thick oven mitts made that impossible. The dish slipped from my hands, hit the edge of the table, and broke apart. Steaming food splattered everywhere.

Davey screamed.

My husband, who was standing near the table, quickly scooped Davey out of his booster seat and rushed him to the kitchen sink. He unbuttoned his pajama top and turned on a gentle stream of cold water to rinse off the scalding food. I watched, horrified, as Davey's burned skin slid away from his chest and arm. We bundled him in clean towels and drove to the community hospital near our home. My body shook uncontrollably as I sat in the car, rocking Davey in my arms. What had I done to my only child, my precious son? *Oh dear God, for this one moment of carelessness, will I lose him?*

The burns on Davey's chest, left arm, and thigh were so severe, the emergency room doctors decided to transfer him to the burn unit at Parkland Hospital, thirty miles away. I rode in the ambulance with Davey. My husband followed in our car, but he was not allowed to enter Parkland's already over-crowded and chaotic emergency room. For the next several hours, I stood next to Davey's ambulance cot in a dazed shock. Fear and dread sat like lead weights in my stomach, and I found it hard to breathe, as if I was struggling to stay afloat in a churning sea of shouting, wailing, hurting people. I stroked my son's baby-fine blond hair and murmured soothing words to comfort him, even though I couldn't stop trembling. The Snoopy balloon my husband had tied to the ambulance cot twirled and bobbed as people brushed past us. Davey's eyes followed the balloon's continual movement, and occasionally, he smiled.

Then I spotted a familiar face in the crowd. It was our pastor. Relief surged through me, and for a short while, my trembling subsided. He prayed with us, and then he told me about a surprisingly similar burn trauma that had happened in his own family. His youngest brother, at the age of four, had scalded himself on his chest and arms when he pulled a pan of boiling water off the kitchen stove. Although his brother's burns eventually healed, our pastor described the emotional turmoil his mother needlessly suffered because she blamed herself for his accident. He truly empathized with me, but I was too consumed with guilt and self-loathing to be comforted. Even if God could forgive me for injuring my son, I would never forgive myself.

Davey was finally admitted to a room in Parkland's burn unit, and my husband rejoined us, accompanied by a social worker. I knew all about child abuse investigations because I had worked as a social worker before my marriage. As she asked me the familiar questions, I lowered my head and answered in a monotone, feeling totally unfit to be any child's mother.

Then she asked Davey to tell her what happened.

"Mommy dropped the dish," he said. Then he turned his wide, blue-eyed gaze on me. "Why did you do that, Mommy?"

I could no longer choke back my tears.

My husband gently wrapped his arm around my shoulders. "It was an accident, Davey. Mommy didn't mean to drop it."

My legs weakened. I sank into the chair next to Davey's bed and covered my face with my hands. *How could my husband still love me after what I had done to our son?*

"Don't cry, Mommy," Davey said. "It was an accident."

I wept even harder. *My precious son was trying to comfort me, after all the pain I had caused him.*

The room went quiet. When my tears were finally spent, I looked up. The social worker was gone.

Davey was placed on antibiotics because infection, always a danger in severe burns, is especially life-threatening to small children. Twice every day, the burn center nurses had to wash his burns thoroughly with antibiotic soap. Since even the lightest touch to his burned skin produced excruciating pain, these baths were sheer torture for Davey. His shrill cries tore right through me. I would have gladly traded places—done anything—to spare him this agony, but there was nothing I could do. I couldn't even pray. I felt horribly ashamed, distanced from God.

For three days, I stayed by Davey's side. I had very little appetite, and although I was exhausted, I could only sleep a few minutes at a time. On that third night at Parkland hospital, I stretched out on the cot beside Davey's bed, but I was too distraught to rest. Vivid images of the accident played over and over in my mind. As I listened to my son's heart-wrenching cries of pain, I seriously considered suicide. I could no longer cope with seeing Davey in such pain—a pain I had caused. And I knew I couldn't bear to live if he died. In desperation, I whispered my first prayer. "Oh God, forgive me. Help me."

Immediately, I felt lifted up, as if by a gentle wind, and my body felt as if it was floating, suspended above the cot. An overwhelming feeling of love wrapped itself around me like a soft, warm blanket. A voice flowed through me, a gentle voice that also held a tone of authority. It said, *You have been forgiven. Be strong for Davey. He needs you now, more than ever.*

I am with you. I will never leave you. Trust Me. For another few moments, the comforting warmth stayed with me. I felt calm, secure, as if I were resting like a baby in divine loving arms. Then slowly and tenderly, the arms released me.

I was lying on the cot in Davey's darkened hospital room, and I could still hear his soft cries. Outside his room, I heard the echo of quick footsteps and the muffled voices of nurses as they passed. Somewhere down the hall, a patient shouted and moaned. Nothing had changed. Except me.

Instead of being tortured by remorse, I felt an inexplicable peace. Hope had replaced despair. My focus had shifted from how I had failed Davey, to how I could help him through this. I had no idea what the future held, but God's loving presence had strengthened me. I would do whatever I could to help my son, and I would trust God with the outcome.

The following day, Davey's doctor told us that the second degree burns on his chest and left arm would heal in several months, with the proper care, but the third degree burn on his thigh might eventually need a skin graft. Davey remained in the burn unit for another seven days. Just before he was released, the nurses taught me how to properly bathe and care for him. More than anything, I wanted him to come home, but I dreaded the prospect of giving him those painful baths twice a day. Worry soon overshadowed the peace that had lingered deep inside me.

Davey's first bath at home was a nightmare. He didn't want to be bathed, so my husband had to kneel next to me so he could hold Davey still in the bathtub. As soon as I gently touched his raw, burned skin with the soft gauze washcloth, Davey flinched, waved his arms, and screamed, "Stop, Mommy, stop! It hurts!" My husband struggled to calm him.

I broke out in a cold sweat. *Why was God punishing me like this? Hadn't I caused my son enough suffering?* I prayed for the strength to continue. I asked God to guide my hands, to help me to wash the burns thoroughly enough to remove the germs, yet gently enough to leave the new, healing skin intact. Somehow, we finished Davey's bath that evening. After my husband and I re-bandaged his burns, we settled him into bed.

When we walked into the kitchen, I was still shaking and my husband looked pale. My mother, who had come to help, poured fresh coffee for me. I sat at the table and reached for the mug. Then I froze. It was the coffee mug my husband had given me the previous Mother's Day, decorated with hearts and the phrase: WORLD'S GREATEST MOM. I pushed the mug away and covered my face with my hands, but I was too exhausted to cry.

The dreaded baths continued, twice a day, for four long months. And as I witnessed the gradual healing process—the slow growth of healthy skin as the raw, burned areas disappeared—I began to view Davey's burn care in a new light. These daily baths weren't a punishment. They were a way, graciously provided by God, for me to help Davey to get well. His burns, caused by my carelessness, eventually healed under my care. The third degree burn on his thigh didn't even need a skin graft.

Dave is twenty-seven now. His burn scars have faded, as

well as his memory of the experience. But I remember with crystal clarity God's merciful answer to my desperate prayer in the hospital room. His supernatural, loving presence filled me with peace and helped me to move past my despair. When I trusted God, He gave me the strength and perseverance I needed to handle the challenging job of Davey's burn care. And as God enabled my hands to cleanse and heal my son's physical wounds, His divine grace healed my emotional wounds.

2

ANGEL IN SCRUBS

SUE TORNAI

Slumped in a chair outside my daughter's hospital room, I buried my head in my hands. The tears began to flow. My mind raced through the events of the past week. Something was wrong with the baby my daughter Janell carried. His lungs had not developed, and surgeons had attempted to correct the problem during fetal surgery, with no success. After the procedure, the waiting began—waiting for Luke to be born. When Janell slept, I walked the halls of the maternity ward or sat in the cold, hard chair in her room. After staying with her a week, getting little or no rest, I was convinced that a person had to be sick to sleep in a busy hospital.

One night when I actually fell asleep in the uncomfortable chair, the bright overhead lights flashed on, and at least ten doctors rushed into the room. "Janell! Roll over!" they exclaimed. They worked with her to change her position. Then they left as quickly as they came. Dazed, I grabbed one of the doctor's coats as she retreated. She turned toward me.

"What happened?" I asked.

"Luke's heart stopped beating, and we thought Janell had rolled over on his umbilical cord," she said. "As soon as we turned her, Luke's heart rate returned to normal."

"Oh, thank you."

Janell resumed her peaceful sleep, but I stayed awake until breakfast. I thanked God for His watchful care through the monitoring devices in Janell's room, for modern medicine and caring doctors and nurses who worked around the clock to save women and babies.

A couple of times the doctor gave Janell drugs to stop her contractions in an effort to delay Luke's birth. He wanted both mother and baby to recover from the procedure and for Luke's lungs to grow. The drug made Janell feel like she was burning from the inside out, so I bathed her in ice water to relieve her suffering.

Weary, after a few days, I longed to get cleaned up.

"Use my shower," said Janell.

"That's for you."

"I'm not using it." Janell smiled.

Standing under the warm water, my anxiety flowed down the drain. The floral sent of the shower gel and shampoo refreshed me. Before I finished drying and styling my hair, Janell's dad, stepmother, brother, and aunt came to visit. They were dressed to do the town, and I felt a little embarrassed— no, a whole lot embarrassed. My hair was half done. The jeans and sweater I wore had suitcase wrinkles. Yet, I felt guilty thinking about my appearance when I considered all Janell had been through.

Our family drew together during this troublesome time. We reminisced of times gone by and toasted with sparkling cider to Janell's healing and Luke's birth. We looked to the future with mixed emotions over the obstacles and hopes for a healthy mom and baby.

After the others left, I went downstairs to the cafeteria for something to eat and took time to make phone calls. People at home, at church, and across several states prayed for Janell and Luke. I called with updates as often as possible. When I returned to Janell's room, she was asleep. Exhausted, I sat outside her room and sobbed out of control. A sweet voice said, "What's the matter?"

"I'm so tired," I cried, "but I need to be strong for Janell."

The nurse brought me a glass of water.

"Thank you." I looked into her smiling face and thought I saw an angel.

"Would you like to stretch out on a sofa?"

Not sure I heard right, I asked, "What do you mean?"

"We have a delivery room that's not in use. You could rest in there, but if someone comes in tonight to have a baby, I would have to ask you to leave."

Tears of relief rolled down my cheeks. "That would be wonderful," I said. My angel led me down the hall and into a large, nicely furnished living room. It was like entering another world. No drapes covered the beauty of the city lights. They looked like millions of diamonds sparkling in the dark sky. Too tired to enjoy the heavenly view, I stretched out on the sofa, and my angel pulled a blanket over me. For the first time in a week, I rested. The sounds of the busy hospital failed to penetrate my peace, and I fell asleep thanking God for the thoughtfulness of a nurse. I awoke to light coming through the morning fog, grateful for a few hours' rest. I looked for my angel to say, "Thank you," but could not find her. Soon I was by Janell's side again.

"Where have you been, Mom?" she asked.

I smiled and told her about my angel, the heavenly lights against the night sky, and a sofa where I slept for a while.

"I'm glad," she said.

"Me, too."

Although doctors tried to delay contractions with modern medicine, there was no stopping Luke. He was born a week after the disappointing surgery.

Today when I see my healthy ten-year-old grandson, I remember his fragile beginnings—fetal surgery and major surgery five days after his birth. He was born without a diaphragm so surgeons relocated his liver and intestines, and installed a patch—an artificial diaphragm, which has been flexible enough to grow with him all these years. Scotty, Luke's dad, says, "I don't know how anyone can look at our boy and not believe in God."

I treasure the memory of how God showed me His love the week before Luke was born. He demonstrated His grace through the compassion of an angel in scrubs. Her sweet smile, soft voice—her simple gifts of a drink of water and a quiet place to rest—inspire me to look for ways I might share God's love with others myself—a helping hand, a sympathetic ear, an encouraging word, or a prayer for a friend in need. Just maybe, I could be somebody's angel too.

3

HELP IS ON THE WAY

JERI DARBY

My workday ended with a stressful meeting, leaving me tense with a migraine and heart palpitations. The day was not over yet! I stopped to cash my check before the thirty-mile drive to a nearby city to pick up a friend from work—a commitment I was starting to regret. "Bang!" This sound startled me about halfway there, and my car started trembling. It wobbled to the side of the highway, and I realized it was a blowout. Only yesterday a concerned neighbor had warned me that the tire was bald and would soon cause problems. *Why didn't I have that tire changed?* I silently criticized myself, filled with remorse for my tendency to procrastinate.

Though my father was a mechanic, I knew absolutely nothing about cars, not even how to change a flat. The scorching evening sun and humidity only intensified my symptoms. I turned on my emergency flashers and prayed. "God, I need help, but not from just anyone. I need one of your servants to stop." I was confident that someone would offer assistance soon, but I was alone and concerned about safety.

Countless motorcycles, automobiles, and even a police officer zoomed past. Some travelers blew their horns and waved as if taunting me. *People can be so cruel!* I thought. *I don't want your help anyways*, I jeered inwardly, feeling tired and frustrated. I really did want one of God's servants to stop. The sun began to set, and my prayers became more vigilant. I sat locked inside my steaming car feeling overwhelmed. *This is odd*, I thought. No one stopped, though two and a half to three hours passed. This was not a common thing for this area.

Maybe if I get out and go through the motions of attempting to change the tire, someone will offer help, I reasoned. I got out, jerked the trunk up, and rummaged through it for a few minutes. Still, not a single automobile pulled over. I felt invisible. Frustrated with my failed attempt, I climbed back inside, locked the car, and turned on the emergency flashers. In times like these, I longed to be more like my tomboy sister, who could tear a car down and put it back together.

Already weary, I found that my urgent petitions to God were draining me even more. Three hours elapsed while I sat helplessly. It felt more like twenty-four. Hungry and irritated, I grew more restless each moment. This is when I remembered something I had heard in church years ago: "Don't wait until God answers your prayers before thanking Him. After you pray, begin to thank Him for the help that is on the way," the speaker had instructed.

I wandered away from church, and it had been ten years since I attended. Over the past few years, the Lord had been drawing me back. I manufactured flimsy excuses that kept me intending to return. I was grateful for this memory surfacing and acted on it immediately.

"God, I believe You have heard my prayer. Thank You for

the help that is already on the way," I prayed and decided, *I'm not going to utter another word of prayer.* I sat and waited quietly. Just before hopelessness consumed me, a car pulled over and parked in front of me.

"Hello, looks like you need some help," the friendly-looking gentleman said, talking through my half-lowered window. I have since forgotten his name, but I'll never forget his kindness. "I passed you an hour ago. Since then I've been trying to figure out which entrance to take to get back to you. I finally found the right one . . . ," he continued.

Help really was on the way! I realized while thanking God again, inwardly. In a few minutes he had my car jacked. "Where is the lock for your hubcaps?" he asked. I didn't have a clue—I did not know that hubcaps had locks or even what one would look like! We searched everywhere. I felt angry at myself for lacking such basic knowledge. Finally, he located it buried in the glove compartment. My tire was changed in minutes. It took longer than this to find the lock.

"Thank you very much!" I expressed, filled with genuine gratitude as we bid each other farewell. I was excited until I turned the key in my ignition. "O-Oh no-oo!" I muttered. I discovered the prolonged use of my emergency flashers had depleted my battery. *I don't believe this!* I thought, with soaring frustration.

Click, click, click was the only sound when I tried turning the key again. I was flooded with disappointment and ambivalence. *Should I take up more of this kind stranger's time? Maybe I should just wait for someone else.* My mind teetered. Looking at the dusk sky and recalling how long I had already waited, I quickly opened the door and stepped out of the car with an apologetic expression.

"Are you having more problems?" he asked, strolling toward me again. He had such a patient and gentle manner.

"Yes, my battery is dead."

"Do you have any cables?" he inquired.

"No," I answered. He walked a few yards down the highway, scanning the ground for something. I was puzzled.

He returned shortly saying, "I thought I might find a piece of wire to use. Is there somewhere you want me to take you to call a tow truck?" This was BCP (before cell phones). I identified a nearby location, and he agreed to drive me there.

While gathering my belongings, I prayed for safety. I was anxious and exhausted and just wanted to get home. While he escorted me to his car, my memory was jolted to a recent media release about a missing woman. Her abandoned car had been found on the side of the road, her picture aired repeatedly to solicit information from viewers. After two weeks she still had not been located. A series of such incidents were being reported in different states. My numb body felt like it was moving in slow motion. A similar news release was broadcasting in my head—only this time I was the missing victim.

"I've been watching oncoming traffic, and it's been slow," he spoke, breaking my trance. He drove toward the lane used for oncoming traffic merging onto the freeway.

I'm dead, I thought. *This guy is a lunatic!* I had never witnessed anything like this before. My thoughts raced as my body tensed through the ordeal. Driving slowly while on-coming traffic blew their horns to alert that he was going the wrong way, he smiled and calmly raised his hand to them, ac-knowledging their concern, and carefully proceeded. He acted like there was nothing unusual.

I barely breathed as he drove until the lane finally ended on a familiar highway, and I discovered I was only a few blocks from the place that I had requested to be taken. "Thank You!" I softly proclaimed to God, as my helper drove into the res-taurant's parking lot. I sighed with relief, and the weight of the day's venture began falling from my shoulders. He maintained his kind and gentle demure until the end.

"Please accept this for your time and inconvenience," I said, extending my hand with a crumpled twenty-dollar bill. Initially I had a large sum of cash with me and feared being robbed, but by this time I would have happily relinquished everything I had just to get home.

His eyes locked with mine, and he replied, "No, take it and put it in church on Sunday." This stranger had no way of knowing that I had strayed away from church and God had been trying to get my attention. Then he added, "I'm just a *servant of the Lord*." These were the last words he spoke to me, and they pierced my heart. The quality of his voice had changed. It was strange and reminded me of the scripture in Revelation 1:15 describing a voice sounding like "many wa-ters." The aftertaste of what had just transpired led me to feel that this was no ordinary man.

I have often reflected on this encounter. I waited a long

time for help and many people passed me by, but it was worth the wait. God is faithful and did exactly what I requested by sending one of *His* servants. I did go to church that Sunday and wept as I placed the twenty dollars in the offering. This visit was the beginning of healing my broken relationship with God.

Whenever I'm in a season of waiting for answers from God, this scenario reemerges in my mind. It serves as a reference when life feels hopeless and answers to prayers seem long overdue. I continue to thank God for His answers because even before they manifest I endeavor to believe that help *is* on the way.

4

A MESSENGER FROM GOD

LORETTA MILLER MEHL

My mother, age ninety-two, suffered a life-threatening illness and was rushed to a hospital shortly after my husband, Bill, and I arrived in Arkansas for a visit. Her condition was deemed terminal, but it was impossible to predict how long Mama might linger. I was drawn in two opposite directions. I felt that I should stay there, but I had promised my husband to attend the Navy reunion in St. Louis. We had already driven from Oregon—more than two thousand miles, on our way to the event. I asked Bill if he would go without me, but he pleaded, "Please come with me. We made this trip so that both of us could attend." Reluctantly, I agreed to go.

We had made personal friends in the group of WWII veterans and their wives over the many years of reunions and were greeted heartily by the people we knew well. The festivities continued as we welcomed each person, sharing stories and meeting at restaurants, shopping, and planning activities for visiting the local sights.

Two days after our arrival, we entered our hotel room to find the message light flashing on the telephone. Without preamble the voice mail from my sister-in-law was short and heart-rending. My mother had died before I could rush back to her bedside for a final good-bye.

We could not leave until morning. I tossed and turned in bed as sleep eluded me. I finally took my daily journal to the bathroom, turned on the light, and wrote about my mother. The words flowed easily as I told about her life, the hardships she had suffered, and her greatest asset, that of loving her friends and family unconditionally. Having poured out my heartfelt feelings on paper, I finally slept.

My husband was reluctant to leave after such a short stay, but his friends convinced him I needed to be with my bereaved siblings. We arose early the next morning, packed our things, and called for a bellhop. The African American man who responded was older than the other attendants who had helped us on arrival. His words were gentle. "No need to hurry. Take all the time you need."

As we left our room, a young girl from the housekeeping staff asked, "How are you today?" I responded, "We're leaving early. My mother has died." Her face filled with compassion as she met my eyes. "Things will get better," she said, "for the Lord will help you." Her words eased my sorrow.

On the way to the garage, Bill spoke to our assistant, explaining that he was worried about finding the route for the return trip out of the city. The man explained what streets to follow and the turns that we should make as we looked for the route numbers. When we arrived in the parking lot, he loaded our luggage then removed his heavy working gloves. Reaching out to us, he said, "Before you go, I would like to pray with you."

We were astonished and grateful. As we stood in a small circle with hands joined, he asked God's guidance in finding our route, for comfort in my loss, for strength in doing whatever was necessary upon my arrival back at my girlhood home. The earnest petitions were for our exact needs to be met for whatever might lie ahead.

My tears flowed throughout the prayer. My husband handed the man a tip, which he tried to refuse, and thanked him. "No stranger has ever prayed for us as you have just done. We will never forget you."

I glanced at the nametag that bore the single word *Arthur*. I said, "You have the same name as my father!" The soothing voice replied, "Now that you know my name, you can pray for me."

I asked, "Arthur, are you a minister?" The man replied, "Yes, I am."

As we thanked him again and my tears continued, he had one final bit of advice for me, words that I so needed to hear. "Now," our helper said, "go rejoicing that your mother is now with the Lord."

We had been apprehensive about finding our way on the return trip, for the route to the hotel had been difficult to locate. Leaving the city, we followed the instructions we were given. At every turn we found the route number clearly marked, as if placed there especially for us.

When Daddy died two years previously, I felt sad that no one gave a personal eulogy about his life. I did not want this to happen at Mama's funeral. So, I talked to my husband and shared my concern about this with him.

"If anyone is going to speak," he replied, "you're the one who will have to do it."

My family and friends knew I had a great tendency to cry during emotional moments. They were astonished on the day of the memorial service when I approached the podium to give the eulogy. My first request was that the people pray for me as I spoke, asking that whatever I said be used to glorify God and honor my mother.

I was mindful that people were praying for me, and I thought of the ministering attendant whose prayers for my husband and me had been answered so fully. I only faltered once when I burst into tears and said, "I was afraid that this might happen, but my husband, Bill, reassured me that 'It's okay if you cry.'" As I finished the final words about the amazing grace of Jesus, I made my way back to my seat with sobs and tear-filled eyes.

Many people spoke to me afterward, saying, "I don't know how you were able to pay such loving tribute to your mother without being overcome with emotion."

I thought I knew. Later, I wrote to the minister who had been sent to me in my grief. "Surely your prayers, along with those who were present, lifted me up and allowed me to speak."

God sent His messenger to bless and reassure me, bringing me comfort and help when I needed it most.

PART 2

GOD'S PROTECTION

5

THE LAST SECOND

JACK TAYLOR

When you're on a motorcycle and coming head-to-head with a full-sized passenger bus, both of you traveling in excess of 100 mph, it gets your attention. Especially when a sheer drop-off is to your left and bumper-to-bumper traffic is coming at you on your right.

There was no question I was in the correct lane, but it was hard to convince the Kenyan bus driver gearing up in the middle of the fog and rain on the escarpment highway at almost nine thousand feet. His windshield was likely as fogged over as my helmet visor. But without a doubt I knew that he was coming my way fast.

For this one moment in time, this situation seemed worse than when an angry elephant charged me, or when I was a horn's width away from a protective mother rhino, or when I was racing for my life in the papyrus rushes ahead of a hippo bent on vengeance.

It had all started forty minutes earlier when I discovered that one of my twenty-eight dorm boys had missed the choir bus. It had been his dream to be on that tour to share the good news of Jesus, and he was left on the muddy campus of the Rift Valley Academy while the rain streamed down.

Andrew begged me to give him a lift on the back of my Honda 185, and we set out winding up the tight turns and steep climbs of the road to the highway. The fog and rain made things difficult to see through the visor once we got onto the road. The red muck flowing across the road gave off an earthy odor, and the diesel exhaust of the groaning trucks and buses reached into my nostrils to irritate my lungs.

A few close calls from vehicles doing a speed run down the country's lone highway toward Nairobi kept things tense. Vans and trucks and buses and cars of all shapes and sizes were pushing along the thin ribbon of potholed tarmac overlooking the Great Rift Valley. Few other motorcycles were traveling the stretch of road in this extreme weather.

I'd had significant troubles on this road before. On a car trip to town early one morning with my wife and three young children, two tires had been destroyed on a single series of rain-filled potholes. Carjackers were known to frequent this area, and travel alone was discouraged. With such short notice I hadn't told anyone what I was doing, and the impulsiveness of my decision was now about to demand a reckoning.

It was the moment with the oncoming bus only hundreds of feet away where my salvation mattered. If I was going to be screen splatter on that bus, I knew that I had asked the Lord Jesus to take control of my life and to use me for His glory. I had full confidence in His promise that His death on the cross had brought about the forgiveness of my sins. I was a new creation in Him, and I had no fear about eternity. Only the terror of the bus getting larger and larger and faster and faster disturbed my settledness.

Of course, it did not help that, as we got even closer to the bus, Andrew wrapped his hands around my throat and squeezed. He was completely freaked out, but there was no way to free my hands so that I could free my throat. The bike would not work well if the driver went unconscious. All I had to offer while facing the front of a bus and the hands at my throat was a quick prayer. "Lord, help!"

So often I was certain it was the prayer of those who remembered me daily that kept us going. Prayer through years of drought, times of serious illness, coup attempts, and blood-drenched election riots, moments of soul-wrenching efforts to make a difference in lives that needed Jesus. More than ever I needed those prayers right now.

The bus wasn't turning, the cars weren't creating space, and the empty chasm on my left side seemed to be imitating the Grand Canyon. Without understanding why, at the last second, I lurched the bike to the left side of the road. A small lip less than six feet wide jutted out along that shoulder for less than one hundred feet. The tires caught the mud patch by the shoulder and my bike left its trail at the very start of that lip and emerged at the very end.

If God had allowed that incident at any other section of road, I'd be a carcass on the side of the road along with the donkeys and dogs and zebras that didn't move quickly enough. If we had gone over the edge, who knows how long it would be before we were discovered. At the last second, a way out was given.

Unfortunately, Andrew was still closing off my throat, and I had to steady the bike with one hand and try to pry his fingers away with the other. My efforts seemed to panic him even more, but he eventually released his hold and returned his hands to my waist. There was no time to slow down and debrief how close we'd come to moving into eternity.

By God's grace we caught the choir bus as it reached the edge of town. If anyone had a fresh testimony of God's mercy and grace, it was a tenth-grade boy named Andrew and a missionary dorm parent named Jack.

Flashes of the funerals and hospitals I had visited crept through my mind. Other missionaries had ended their testimonies in different ways in this African country. The tombstones bore witness that a life's work does not always end up with a hero's welcome home on this planet.

The ride home in the torrential downpour was a lot more controlled and meditative. There were other accidents and other carnage that day along the road between Nairobi and Naivasha, but I thank God I was no more than a witness.

Over the years I've been privileged to share my life with thousands of missionary kids such as Andrew and to see that God was not yet finished with me when He brought me face-to-face with a bus on the escarpment highway in Kenya.

6

ANGELS ON DUTY

MARLENE ANDERSON

The kids were down for the night. I finished the dishes and shut off the kitchen lights. As I moved through the dark hallway and entranceway to the living room, I felt an uncomfortable unease.

An open stairway wound from our home's entrance to the second floor. *What if someone was on the stairwell? They could jump out at me in the dark. Why am I walking through the house in the dark anyway?* Was it truly too much trouble to have to go back and shut off lights?

I just have an overactive imagination, I assured myself. *No one is in my house except three sleeping children in their bedrooms upstairs.*

I hurried through the dark entranceway and felt an immediate sense of relief and safety when I flicked on the living room lights. Yet, I was glad the piano was at the opposite end of the room. I wanted to be as far as possible away from the semi-dark entranceway. I sat down and started to play.

My husband was a musician. During the day he chaired the music department at a local community college. Five nights a week he led an eight-piece band and directed a musical show at a local hotel. Many musicians in the band were teachers, bakers, postmen, or bank executives during the daytime, all coming together in the evening to do what they loved most—playing their instruments.

Like other musicians' wives, I spent many nights alone. My husband and I built our three-story house in a rural suburb. Across the street from our home was a large undeveloped section of land, overgrown with trees and underbrush that had well-worn paths leading to a neighboring community college.

It was a friendly wood, and we loved to walk through it, enjoying a bit of natural habitat in the middle of a growing neighborhood population. Yet, at night, even the friendliest of places can take on a less welcoming—perhaps even sinister—atmosphere.

It was summer; the night was warm, and the sliding deck door next to our baby grand piano was open. I could see my neighbor's house beyond my backyard. A dog barked. *How silly I am*, I chided myself. Pushing aside any lingering fears, I convinced myself it was beyond silly to think that someone had entered the house while I was in the kitchen working.

What was that? With my heightened awareness I thought I heard a noise. My hands paused on the keyboard as I glanced toward the entranceway. Was that a shadow moving toward the door? I couldn't see the stairs, only the front door.

In my bravest voice, I called out boldly, "Hello—is anyone there?" I thought how stupid that sounded as I heard myself speak. If I wasn't careful, I would wake the kids.

Silence.

All right, if I was going to put this niggling fear to rest, I would have to go investigate. I picked up a hymn book and started toward the entranceway. I figured I could bash any intruder over the head with it. Just before I reached the entranceway, and before I could see the stairs, a figure jumped out at me.

"Yes, there is!"

Time froze as the world slowed to a stop. His hair was blond, long, and scraggly. He must have been in his early twenties. There was the stubble of an unshaven face. His eyes were blue and cloudy. In an instant, instinct spun me around to run. But before I could take more than two steps, his judo chop knocked me flat and he had twisted one arm behind me as his knees sank into my lower back.

Someone had just poured an ice-cold bucket of water on me—or so it felt. Stone-cold, hard reality struck through my consciousness. I was alone. The kids were asleep. My husband wouldn't be home for hours. The neighbors had not heard. There was no one to help me. There was only me—and him.

Frantically my mind raced. What should I do? I remembered reading an article in the latest edition of *Guideposts* the week before about a woman who had been abducted, and how she was able to talk her way out of her situation. It was the only weapon I had. I decided to try it. I had nothing to lose.

"Don't you know that God loves you?" *What exactly had she said?* "There is no need to do this." *I don't think these are the right words*. My fear had given way to a laser-sharp focus of the present moment. The knee in my lower back hurt, and I could smell the stench of beer on his breath. (For a long time afterward, whenever I smelled beer I became nauseous.)

"Come on." The words were coarse, filled with an alcoholic bravado. With one arm around my neck and the other pinning my right arm behind my back, he shoved me through the dining room and kitchen toward the back of the house. As we reached the laundry room adjacent to the kitchen, he stopped and began to fumble with my blouse.

Big mistake! *Oh no, you don't*, the words screamed in my head. With a strength and determination born from the desperation of the moment, I wrenched away from him and yanked open the back door. But before I could open the screen door, he caught up with me.

I didn't make it.

Then a strange thing happened. Instead of grabbing me and closing the door, he said in a shaky, scared, and childlike voice, "Okay, if you will let me go, I'll go."

If I let him go, he'll go? That was the dumbest thing I'd ever heard. I wasn't holding him. He had been holding me! But I acted upon this as though a script had been put in place, and with a powerful, authoritative voice replied, "Okay. Get out of my house, and don't ever come back!" I held the screen door open as he dashed through and into the night.

With shaking hands, I quickly locked the door, throwing the deadbolt and turning on every light in the house as I quickly made my way to the office to dial 911.

"911—may I help you?"

"Yes, someone has just broken into my house and tried to attack me. I am all right and he has left, but I would like the police to come and check to see if he is still around." I don't know where I found the will and stamina, but I found myself speaking calmly and clearly as I gave the operator my address and the details of what had just happened.

She quickly contacted different police agencies that might service our area. Portland police—sorry, they were out of our jurisdiction. Tigard police—no, same thing. The dispatcher was getting angry and frustrated. "I will get someone out there if I have to come out myself," she said.

"It's all right," I reassured her. "The doors are locked, and I don't think he will be able to get back in the house. I will try to reach one of my neighbors in the meantime." In a crisis it seemed I was always reassuring everyone else.

Finally, the county police agreed to send someone out as soon as possible. I assured the 911 operator that I would be okay, and then I called my husband at the hotel. The bartender of the huge lounge where the band was playing picked up the phone.

"Hi, I am Marlene Anderson and my husband is leading the band there. Are they in the middle of a show?"

"Yes, but they should take a break in about five minutes."

"Okay, would you please have him call me as soon as he is finished? Someone broke into our home and attacked me. I'm safe and okay, and the police are on their way so don't interrupt him during the show. I just wanted to let him know. Be sure to tell him I am okay."

"I'll get a note to him immediately," replied a very concerned bartender.

Later, I was told my husband's face turned chalk-white when he read the note. He told a band member to take over the band as he bolted out the door. In fact, although he was over eight miles away, he arrived before the police. It was the only time I ever saw my even-tempered husband angry enough to hurt someone.

It was only as I relayed the events of the evening to both the police and my husband that I realized the situation could have ended much worse. My whole body started shaking as the shock wore off and the pain in my neck let me know just how hard I had been hit.

How did the man gain entrance into our home without my knowledge? Although I usually was methodical in locking all the doors when my husband left for work, this night I had left the front door unlocked. The intruder watching from the woods across the street quietly entered the house after my husband left. He was probably halfway up the stairs when I shut off the lights to go into the living room. He had remained hidden as I passed through the entranceway. I shudder to think of the terror I would have felt if he had attacked me in the dark. When I heard noises at the piano, he probably was having second thoughts and was going to sneak out the door.

But the question still remained. Why was he so scared and shaken up? Although I don't remember every detail, I know that the intruder still had the upper hand. The neighbors hadn't heard anything. Something or someone had scared him—badly. And I knew then that God had sent an angel to intervene. We don't always see the angels God sends, but upon reflection we can see the evidence of their presence.

They never caught the intruder. And it took a long time, the purchase of a German shepherd, and the installation of an alarm system to calm my anxiety when my husband left for work. I no longer played the piano or sang at night but chose to work in a brightly lit sewing room with instant access to a phone.

I also learned to pay attention to my fears even when they might seem irrational. But even more important, I was reminded again that God will be with me in whatever circumstances I find myself. His angels are always on duty.

7

MY SPECIAL ANGEL

MAX ELLIOT ANDERSON

It was one of those happy occasions for which my family prepared to gather. Our son, Jim, was graduating. For us, this wasn't just any graduation. He was going to walk across the stage and receive his diploma from law school.

"Can you believe how fast the last three years have gone by?" I asked.

"Fast for you, Dad," he said with a smile.

My eighty-seven-year-old mother was making the three-hour trip into Chicago, with the help of my sister. Sarah, Jim's younger sister, had flown from Orlando, into Midway Airport, a fact that will become more important later.

During one of the times my son and I drove over to pick up family members from their hotel, I asked, "Tell me about the new surveillance cameras all over the city."

He shook his head. "Some people don't like them. They call it more of Big Brother."

Because of his law interests, I continued, "What's your opinion?"

"There was a lot of opposition," he told me, "but now people like them."

"What changed their minds?"

He pointed to a pole in the next block. "See that flashing blue light?" he asked.

"Yes."

"The mayor started putting those up in high-crime areas. Each one has a video camera that sends pictures back to a command center."

"Are they doing any good?" I asked.

He nodded. "Wherever one of those has been installed, crime goes way down. Now they plan to put up even more of them." He went on to explain that a 911 call activates the camera nearest the call and police can see what's happening.

"Interesting," I said.

During the graduation ceremony, I know I puffed up a little with pride when I heard his name announced and watched my son receive his honors. It was a truly magnificent event.

My mother whispered, with tears in her eyes, "I wish your father could have lived to see this. He would have loved it."

A brief reception followed, then we were off to dinner at a quaint Italian restaurant. The next afternoon, it was time for family members to head back home. Jim, Sarah, my wife, and I began the drive out to Midway Airport, so our daughter could make her return flight to Florida. For anyone who is unfamiliar with this airport, it is located on the extreme southwest side of Chicago.

Along the way, we passed some of the public housing projects where life can become so desperately difficult for those who have few other options. You might say that our family tended to stand out in these surroundings.

As we passed under a railroad bridge, I heard what sounded like the hissing of an industrial air compressor at a construction site.

"What was that?" my wife asked in alarm from the backseat.

Just then our Explorer began to sway. Immediately I knew we were in trouble.

"It's a flat," I answered, guiding the car to the curb. By this time, the rear tire on the passenger side flapped uselessly on its rim.

"Now what do we do?" Sarah asked. "I'll miss my flight."

Quickly my eyes darted as I assessed the situation. With my previous military training and working as a film and video producer, I've traveled to some of the world's most violent hot spots. I know a dangerous situation when I see one, and this . . . was dangerous.

"We'll get Sarah a cab," I said. "You two go with her to the airport and be sure she makes her flight. I'll figure out the spare." In a flash, they were gone, and I was left alone. I'd never changed a tire on our Explorer before and was I in for a treat. The spare is located under the car. It has to be let down with a crank by a pulley system.

A man from the neighborhood approached me from the side. "Need any help?" he asked. "I can change it for you."

But something about the way he looked at me set off a warning bell in my head.

"No thanks," I answered. "I've got it."

A woman sitting at the bus stop called out, "You can't

leave your car there." She pointed in the same direction that my family had gone. "There's a gas station a few blocks that way. They can help."

After another brief scan of the area, I decided there was no way I was leaving my car, unattended, in this neighborhood. "Thank you," I said.

I climbed back behind the wheel, pulled off the main street, and into the entrance to one of the housing projects. It was a one-way street, going the wrong way. I eased into that drive, turned around, and pointed my car in the right direction. Then I moved up as close to the intersection as I could, in order to make sure I would be as visible as possible. Immediately another vehicle, from the projects, pulled in behind me.

"Lord," I prayed, "I'm in trouble here, and I sure could use Your help. Thank You."

"You shouldn't be here," the woman warned, as she stepped out of her car. "Don't you know where you are?"

"Yes," I responded with confidence.

"Do you know how to change your tire?"

"Not yet." I held up the vehicle manual. "Reading about it right now."

"Well," she demanded, "you can't stay here."

Another woman hurried out from an apartment. She had a frightened look in her eyes, as she walked straight toward me. "You have got to get out of here," she urged. "It's too dangerous."

"Well, I'm not going anyplace," I said as we looked down

toward the curb. "Not with a flat like that."

"Are you alone?" she asked.

Again one of those warning bells went off. "No. My son is with me. He'll be back in a few minutes."

She looked around. "Your son?"

I nodded. "He's coming right back."

Her look softened. "That's good. But you have to get back in your car until he does. There's people who will come up and take everything you have. It's not safe for you here."

"Thank you," I told her. "I will."

She turned to go back to the car behind me, then stopped, turned around, and walked back. "You *will* stay in your car?"

"I will."

"Good. Then, when your son gets back, one of you can work on the tire and the other can watch out. If anything happens, you just call 911, and the police will come in a few seconds. They always do when we call."

She hesitated for a moment longer. A broad smile came across the face of this ebony angel. "God bless you," she said and climbed into her car. Then the two women drove away.

As she had warned, I got back into my car and began reading the manual. But something made me look out the front window. When I did, I noticed, high up on a pole, right in the intersection where I sat, a bright, blue flashing light, from one of those video surveillance cameras. It sent out its warning beam like a lighthouse on a stormy night. And it felt like my lighthouse in the midst of this storm.

Soon my wife and son returned. As they climbed out of

the cab, my daughter called from the airport to see if I was all right. With my son as a lookout, I began the task of lowering the spare. There were some complications, concerning where I could set the jack, because of how the tire sat on the rim. This caused the change to take twice as long.

While I was working, a housing authority truck drove out of the projects and stopped next to us. The driver lowered his window only a few inches. His rolled-up sleeve revealed a barbed-wire tattoo.

"You people know where you are?" he asked in a gruff voice.

"We're beginning to," I said with a slight laugh.

He kept his street-tough look and tone. "You keep your eyes open," he warned, "and get out of here as fast as you can." Then he drove off.

I picked up the pace, realizing I had already been in this spot far longer than I should. Finally I was able to get the spare on and began tightening the bolts. That's when another car drove into the one-way street the wrong way and stopped in front of my car. A man, who, like us, clearly wasn't from the area either, stepped out, and walked over to where I was working.

"Do you people know where you are?" he asked in alarm.

"We do now," I said.

"You can't stay here."

"You're about the sixth person to tell me that," I said with a sigh.

"Well, it's true." He pointed across the street. "There used

to be a gas station on that corner. There were so many robber-
ies and murders, they had to tear it down."

"Really?" I asked.

"Really! I just stopped because you people looked so out of
place in this neighborhood. I wanted to make sure you understood how dangerous it is. You need to get going right away."

We talked as I hurried to finish my work, and I found
that he was a pastor, with a radio program on WMBI in Chicago. We traded business cards, and then he was on his way. I
loaded the flat tire in the back and tossed my tools on top of
it. That's when I noticed a huge gash in the tire. This surprised
me because I hadn't seen or heard anything hit us before the
tire went down. We slammed our doors, locked them, and
sped away from the curb. As I turned back onto Cicero Av-
enue, my eyes were drawn to the flashing blue light again.

"Thank You, Lord," I prayed silently. God had reminded
me that He was there, watching over us, protecting us, whenever we call out to Him.

After we had returned home, I drove my car to the tire
store to have the flat replaced. While I was sitting in the waiting room, a man came out of the garage. "Want to see what
was inside your tire?" he asked.

"Sure."

He held out a large piece of angle iron, too large I thought
to ever have penetrated my tire. "Let me see that," I said as I
reached out for it. In disbelief I told him, "I'm keeping this.
No one would believe it if I didn't."

Though I'm confident that some of "Chicago's Finest"

were watching over me by video, in that dangerous neighborhood, I also believe that I had help from someplace higher and from my very special angels who stopped to warn me.

8

SHE'S OUT OF CONTROL

LORRAINE M. CASTLE

The scream pierced the silence in sharp contrast to the early spring morning stillness that had been kissed by the dew and predawn rain. I was spinning out of control. My hands left the steering wheel, and I squeezed my temples in a fruitless attempt to quiet the tsunami that flooded my soul. *Overwhelmed* is not an adequate word to describe how I felt as what moments before had been normal now riveted out of control.

Although the gearshift was in the Drive position, the car spun around, thrown into Reverse as though it had a mind of its own. Facing forward, I looked into the rearview mirror and watched as greater distance was placed between my original destination and me. As I had so many times in my lifetime, I was going the wrong way and watching my future disappear.

I was on a four-lane highway at the height of the morning rush hour in the midst of Center City. I watched as cars that seconds before were within immediate impact, appeared to evaporate into the atmosphere while my car and I had become a single missile rushing toward an unknown destination.

I continued to gaze into the rearview mirror that now held my destiny. In milliseconds, I revisited my life. Up to that point, I feared death. Now I was comforted as the hand of a loved one who had passed away caressed my shoulder with a touch that felt as soothing as a perfumed wisp of air. Feelings of fear and confusion fused with the realization that I was not in control of the situation. I was unable to will my eyes away from the rearview mirror, as fear melted away and was replaced by a still calm.

The four-lane highway sat in the midst of the largest inner-city park in the United States. Filled with memories, my mind drifted back to happier, carefree times as we rode in the back of a green pickup truck on our way to the park for a family picnic. Surrounded by loved ones as I laughed and played, I was oblivious to the darkness that the world around me held. Would this park that was filled with so many happy memories now become the foundation for my epitaph?

My car, propelled into reverse, sped across four lanes of traffic, bounced up onto the curb, and skated across the cement pavement. The grass briefly slowed the momentum until the surface gave way to the muddy remnants of the dew and the last evening's rain, relaunching the car into an uncontrolled missile.

This was the same grass that we barbecued on so many years ago, laughing and playing with my favorite uncles as my aunt and mother laid out mouth-watering salads and desserts that would be devoured by all in a matter of minutes. This was the same grass that we ran on, playing tag until we fell onto the soft grass, gasping for air in between the laughter, and gazing at the perfectly blue, cloudless sky above. Would this grass become my final resting place? Would this be my last memory of life on this earth?

Yes. I was out of control. Images of trees, grass, and the Schuylkill River were visible in the rearview mirror, jockeying for attention as my mind raced—filling with past successes, too many failures, and missed opportunities. Panic returned as I realized that I was running out of time.

Thoughts rushed to the previous evening as I recalled filling the tank of my car with gasoline. I was speeding in reverse. I had a full tank of gas. The gas tank was in the rear. And I was out of control. Panic escalated. The touch . . . The panic . . . The touch returned, nudging me with a sense of urgency. I felt a spiritual presence commanding me to fear not.

I screamed again. Again, I heard, "Fear not." My screaming stopped. My focus was drawn away from the rearview mirror. I was out of control. I turned to the One who was in control of my life, the car, and the entire situation. I prayed, "Lord Jesus! Please save me!" I wanted to say more, but there was no time.

Trees continued to race by. The river drew closer. I remembered that I could not swim. I noticed I was no longer screaming. I was waiting. What was I waiting for?

I remembered a nightmare I used to have every September. Later in life, I was told that the nightmare was connected to the anxiety of returning to school and my desire to be the perfect student. The nightmare was one that many experience where someone is chasing them. I run, fall over a cliff, and then I'm rudely jolted out of sleep before reaching the bottom. Every year, it was the same. One year I decided that I wanted the nightmare to end. When I fell over the cliff, I forced myself to stay asleep. I wanted to wake up, but I had to reach the bottom of the cliff. I waited. Eventually, I reached the bottom. I woke up and smiled when I realized that I did not perish from the free-fall. The nightmare did not return the next September. It had been on a permanent vacation for more than forty years.

Back to reality, I waited. I waited for the One who was in control. I didn't know how this would end. But I knew that I was prepared. There was much that I had done in my life. There was much that was yet to be done. In spite of my perceived shortcomings, I was prepared.

My thoughts were interrupted as the car screeched to a complete halt. A tree on the driver's side halted its progression. The steel car collapsed in the same manner as an empty aluminum can of soda that is crushed by a construction worker's shoe. The glass gave way to the pressure of the crash, shattered into hundreds of pieces of varying sizes, and shards of glass were propelled into every imaginable direction. The sounds of crumpling steel and smithereens of glass pierced my eardrums.

Unable to open the door on the driver's side, I slid toward the passenger door and exited the car seconds after the glass shattered. Cars that were previously nonexistent or transparent now rushed by as everyone sped to their respective destinations. No one stopped. How amazing is that? No one stopped, so I waited.

I stood by the crumpled car and waited. Within minutes that felt like hours, a fire chief happened by, passed me, observed the situation, pulled up onto the pavement, put his car into Reverse, and finally came to my rescue.

Unable to find the words, I pointed into the direction of my crushed car. Observing the situation, the fire chief handed me the only thing that he had that could slow the blood that flowed from the left side of my face—a sheet of plain printing paper. Though rough, it brought me comfort. My help had arrived. The fire chief ushered me into his car, and he quickly sped off in the direction of the closest hospital.

I spent the next three hours in the emergency room as the doctor, using tweezers, removed microscopic slivers of glass from my face, eyelids, eyelashes, and hair. Amazingly, not one sliver of glass or debris entered my eyes. It was a miracle.

My car was totaled. Like the tree that stopped the car, I was still standing. I was scarred, but the scars were not permanent. Not one stitch was required. The scars have since faded. I had renewed purpose. Understanding that I was a walking miracle gave me a renewed strength.

My life could have ended on that day. The fact that it occurred on April 1 was no coincidence. That day convinced me that there is a God and that He watches over you and me. On that day, my mind was not on Him, but His mind was definitely on me. On that day, I was reminded that when we yield control to God, He will guide our steps and orchestrate the situation so that He gets the glory. The first step is the most difficult step. Yielding control did not and still does not come easy for me. I am a control freak. However, it is a wonderful feeling to yield the reins of control over to Jesus. Life is wonderful because I know exactly who is in control!

9

A CRY FOR HELP

COLLEEN REECE

And it shall come to pass, that before they call, I will answer;
and while they are yet speaking, I will hear.

ISAIAH 65:24 KJV

It started with five pieces of fabric and a coat. A crimson coat. An honest-to-goodness, first-ever, "store-boughten" coat.

In 1941, most folks in Darrington, our small western Washington logging town, wore hand-made clothes. They were usually cut down from older family members' outgrown garments, turned and pressed by thrifty seamstresses. However, when I was almost six and ready to start school, my parents took me to town to buy material for new dresses. I thought I was in heaven.

Mom told me to choose five pieces of cloth, a different one for each school day. I examined every bolt of fabric in the store, entranced by the crisp, printed material as bright and colorful as our flower garden. At last I chose a rosy pink, a light blue, a pretty green, and a yellow-orange combination. The lavender-flowered material I liked best became my "pansy dress." Total cost with buttons, thread, and trim was only a few dollars. I was all set, except for a winter coat.

In those days, even young children knew how hard it was to come by cash money. Dad worked long hours cutting timber, but the pay was small. I'd been wearing my older brother's outgrown mackinaw, which Mom had cleverly remodeled.

When Daddy told me I'd be getting a "store-boughten" coat, I said, "I don't need a new coat, Daddy. I've got a good coat." He never tired of telling about my response, clearing his throat afterward. Nevertheless, we made an all-day shopping trip to a large town fifty miles away. I ended up with a dark-red wool coat and matching hat that made me feel like a storybook princess.

The next morning, I asked my mother, "Please, may I go show my new coat and hat to Aunt Leathy?" ("Great-Aunt Leathy" was our closest neighbor.) I had to ask several times. For the past few days, Mom's ears had been so stopped up with a bad cold she was almost stone-deaf.

When I finally made her understand, she gave her permission, and off I ran. My feet danced past the shallow sandpit, around the big stump, and down the narrow path (formed from countless small feet tripping over the hard-packed earth) by the huge dogwood tree. Great-Aunt Leathy ooh-ed and ah-ed over my beautiful coat and hat.

Then, filled with joy, I started for home.

Dad's first cousin and her husband lived just down the road from us on the way to Green's Pond, where folks ice-skated in winter. They owned an enormous, mean bull that became so dangerous Herman decided he didn't want the animal around. He sold the bull to some cattle buyers, who came with their truck to haul him away. They had a terrible time loading the bull but finally got him in their open truck. Herman was relieved to see the last of him.

Moments after the new owners pulled away with the maddened bull, he broke free. He leaped out of the truck and charged up the road toward our place, roaring like a hurricane.

Skipping and happy, I had almost reached the big stump when I heard the terrifying noise. I looked up. Two men with rifles stood by their truck, shouting at the top of their lungs, but it was too far away for me to hear what they were saying. *And a huge bull raced straight toward me from the other side of the sandpit.*

Neither of the men fired. Perhaps they were too afraid of hitting me.

I stared at the bellowing beast, more frightened than I had ever been in my entire life. My hands clenched with fear and felt sweaty. What could I do? It was as far back to Great-Aunt Leathy's as to my house. I did the only thing I could: I climbed onto the flat stump and screamed, "*Mama!*"

The bull came closer. I yelled louder.

"Mama, come get me. Mama, I'm afraid!" Even at that young age I knew standing on a stump less than four feet high could not protect me from the maddened bull.

I had no way of knowing God was already working on a plan to rescue me. Mom was washing clothes on her scrub board in the woodshed at the back of the house, too far away to hear me. Yet still the words, "Mama, come get me!" suddenly rang in her ears. She shook her head. Was she dreaming? No. The cry came again. "Mama, I'm afraid! Come get me!"

She dropped the wet garment she was holding and dashed toward the sound of my voice. She saw the crazed bull. Then she saw me.

"Colleen! Run!" Had she shouted or only whispered? She couldn't tell until I turned toward her, so frightened I couldn't move.

She hurtled toward me, reached the stump, and snatched me to the ground. We began our race for life. Mom yanked me along as fast as my fear-inspired feet would go, half-carrying me at times. Our open, empty garage offered no refuge. Mom pulled me around the corner of the building, just as the bull reached the front. "Faster!" Mom screamed. We fled down the path around the backside of the house. The bull snorted and continued his pursuit.

With a final desperate burst of speed, we reached the steps to the small back porch. She jerked me off my feet and pelted up them. The bull tore past. Cheated of his prey, his pounding hooves churned up the open field toward the side road and uprooted good-sized trees in his path of destruction.

We stumbled inside the house and collapsed. "Thank God!" Mom said. We cried together. I don't remember ever being hugged harder than at that moment.

It took hours for the cattle buyers to capture the bull and take him away. Later, one reportedly said, "If that bull had trampled that child, I'd have gotten out of the cattle business."

The most important part of the story was not our incred-ible race against danger and possible death, but that Mom's ears only cleared long enough for her to hear me call. When we reached the safety of our house, they stopped up again!

I am living proof of God's grace. This unmistakable evi-dence of His love strengthened my faith as a child, blessed family and friends, and gave us a foundation on which to build a lifetime of trust in our heavenly Father . . . the Father who cared enough to hear His child's cry and send help in a truly miraculous way.

10

IN THE SHELTER OF HIS WINGS

LINDA VEATH COX

Be merciful to me, O God, be merciful to me!
For my soul trusts in You; and in the shadow of Your wings
I will make my refuge, until these calamities have passed by.

PSALM 57:1 NKJV

I looked at the clock on the wall, willing the hands to move quickly to quitting time. Even though I loved my job, I was ready for the day to be over. And when it was 3:30 p.m. sharp, I was out the door.

It was a beautiful spring day in early June. Farmers were harvesting wheat, and I was looking forward to the drive home past the fields where they were working. I was thankful to live only eight miles from my office at that time and felt like I had the best of both worlds. A short drive home. But a beautiful drive, as well.

Never in my wildest dreams did I anticipate what lay ahead for me that afternoon. We've heard many times that statistics show most automobile accidents occur quite close to home. Well, I was about to find out.

As soon as I reached the part of the highway where the

curves and side roads ended, I would have a straight shot toward home. As I rounded that last curve, I saw a line of cars coming toward me in the other lane.

And somebody trying to pass that whole line of cars. Somebody in a big hurry. I immediately let up on the accelerator, slowing down to give him all the room he needed to get over. But he was making no attempt to move over, nor was anybody slowing up enough to allow him to pull in front of them. Not good.

I slowed even more and he just kept coming. I pulled over as far as I could and still stay on the highway, but he was angling toward me. Was he purposefully trying to hit me? I had to make a choice. A hard one. To leave the highway and drive down an embankment. Or risk hitting him head-on.

I don't remember a lot about the impact, just hearing myself screaming, "Nooooo! He's hitting me." And then I was surrounded by a big, soft white cloud of protection.

My car stopped almost upon impact. It was leaning sharply as it rested on the steep embankment along the side of the road. My face had a burning sensation, but I could also tell that I had no major injuries. Something that looked like smoke was floating in the air over the hood of my car, and I thought it was on fire.

My first instinct was to get out the driver's side door. It didn't budge. As I saw later, that side of the car was totally destroyed. I quickly moved toward the passenger door, which thankfully opened, and I stumbled into the fresh air.

In the short time it took me to get out of the car, a man

had already made it down the embankment to help me. I leaned on him as we made the short climb to the roadside, where he sat down next to me. He talked with me to keep me calm as his wife called 9-1-1. She offered to get my purse and briefcase from the car, an offer I gladly accepted. Another woman sat down on my other side, offering to call someone for me. Because my husband was harvesting wheat, I asked her to call my mother.

While I sat there, I stared numbly at my car. It rested on the part of the embankment that had just been dug up for a water line. It had been dust floating in the air that I had seen, not smoke. The soft dirt had stopped the car quickly, which was why it didn't travel further out of control. Or roll over, where I'd have been trapped inside.

Thankfully the young man driving the other car was okay, but we both went to the hospital to be checked over. Mom was waiting for me in the ER when we arrived and had a stricken look on her face that only a worried mother could have. Other than having to have glass swabbed off my face, I checked out fine.

All I wanted to do was go home, get in the bathtub, and not come out for a very long time. But I needed to call the towing company first so I could make arrangements to get the rest of my belongings from the car. When I told the tow truck driver who I was and what car I was calling about, he said, "Lady, I shouldn't be talking to you. You should be dead or at least in the hospital with major injuries." Wow. Was the damage really that bad? Apparently so. When I saw my car the next day, I realized how blessed I was to have walked away from that wreck.

Yet I just kept beating myself up about whether I could have done something differently to have avoided the wreck completely. My reflexes are not quick, and I feel as if I don't respond well in emergency situations. I had to have missed something that would have prevented it.

I was still fretting about this a few days later as I sat in church on Sunday morning. My pastor had a prayer of thanksgiving for protection on the roads. I was truly blessed to be safe, but I couldn't stop questioning my performance behind the wheel.

As I walked out of the worship service, I was stopped by a man from the church whom I barely knew. He had witnessed the wreck. His words were God-sent: "I want to congratulate you on the way you drove. You did everything you possibly could to avoid that wreck. Good job driving."

The tears finally came as the reality of it all sank in. God had been in every detail of that wreck—protecting me, providing for me, soothing me. The soft dirt that slowed me down. Not rolling over and being trapped by the electric pole. People there immediately to help. My face plastered with bits of glass and not one drop of blood shed. No serious injuries for me or the young man who hit me. The love in the look on Mom's face. The tow truck driver's comments. The "good job" remarks on Sunday. And let's not forget the most important of all—the soft "presence" surrounding me at impact.

Each of those things was stamped with God's love and

grace. No doubt about it.

But there's more to this story. God not only provided for me in that wreck. He also used it as a reminder of His constant protection. You see, I had been working in an office where an ex-employee was a threat to our lives for several years. We had been battling to get procedures in place to protect us from him. The very day of my wreck we received paperwork establishing those procedures. Our office staff had celebrated. Protection at last.

But God reminded me on that fateful drive home that those procedures, while safety precautions, weren't the ultimate protection we needed. The Lord and His multitude of angels had already been providing us with the best refuge anyone could have asked for. I just needed a big "bump" in the road to wake me up to see that.

I carry a photo of my wrecked car in my Bible as a reminder of what God did for me that day. It's something I will never forget. When I start worrying about the future and what might happen, all I have to do is look at that photo. And remember God's grace and protection through a wreck that I never should have walked away from.

Yes, indeed. He truly is our refuge in whatever calamities come our way.

11

BE NOT AFRAID

JAMES BRALEY

As I walked into the private dining room at a well-known Moscow restaurant, I mentally pinched myself to be sure I was awake. I grew up in a very small town in Arizona, and it had seemed like a huge deal when I went away to college in Southern California. Now, here I was in Russia. I remembered how fearful my wife and I had felt on our first mission trip to the former Soviet Union. It was a great unknown for us, filled with imaginings of what could happen to us while we were there. Yet we were sure this opportunity was God's direction for us, so we claimed the promise of God in Isaiah 41:10: "So do not fear, for I am with you; do not be dismayed, for I am your God. I will strengthen you and help you; I will uphold you with my righteous right hand" (NIV). To our amazement we learned that some of the Russian teachers who attended our convocations were equally afraid of us, until we got to know one another.

When communism fell in the Soviet Union, the Russian people were left with nothing to cling to. For years they had been told the Bible was a lie, and Jesus Christ was a myth. Now communism was gone, and they had nothing to believe in and no direction for their lives. Political, religious, and educational leaders of Russia knew great voids needed to be filled, so they approached the Western world for help in teaching Judeo-Christian morals and ethics to the teachers throughout the Soviet states. They believed it was too late for the adults, but they wanted help for their children.

My first awareness of this desire came in September of 1990 while I was in Timisoara, Romania. Following the death of Nicolae Ceausescu in 1989, one of the first things to arise from the ashes of Romania's revolution was a movement to start Christian schools. This would have been forbidden under Ceausescu, so direction was needed to make it possible. Another educator and I were asked to come and train Romanian educators how to start Christian schools. While we were there, Dr. Alexi Brudinov and his assistant, Dr. Olga Polyavoskaya, came by train from Moscow to see me. These two were the heads of the entire Soviet school system, and they came to invite me to Russia to train their teachers how to teach the Bible in their classrooms. "Dr. Brudinov," I said, "I don't know how to teach atheists to teach the Bible." To which he replied, "Then come and teach them to be Christians." I was hooked.

In response to the urgent request from Russian leadership, a group called CoMission was formed from about eighty-five mission agencies, Christian colleges, and Christian associations, and curriculum based on the life of Christ was prepared in record time. When the first group of sixty-five volunteers left for the former Soviet Union, my wife and I were with them.

I had been on several trips already when the dinner at the restaurant took place. On this particular trip I had remained for a two-day planning meeting after the convocations were finished, and our Russian host had provided a bus and driver to take participants to the site of their choice for an evening of relaxation. A missionary couple who lived in Russia invited me to join them at the restaurant, where a demonstration of Russian dances was being given during the dinner hour. From our private dining nook we could walk to a balcony that overlooked the first floor, where the dances were taking place. After watching the entertainment, we started back to our table, but I decided to use the restroom before our dinner arrived. I went down a flight of stairs to the first floor, where the restroom was located.

The restroom was nicely appointed, with a foyer where sinks and mirrors were located. The facilities were in another room behind the foyer. When I entered the foyer, two Russian men were there, washing their hands. When I came out of the back room, the two men were still there, but one of them was kneeling in front of the exit door. He made no sign of moving, but I kept walking toward him, thinking he would get up. Still he didn't move. I remember thinking that maybe if I bumped his foot he would move. Then I suddenly realized the second man was behind me, poking something into my back and trying to get my backpack open. I was truly in trouble.

To this day I cannot tell how it happened, but the next thing I knew I was outside the restroom, facing the entry door. My backpack was intact, and my passport and other papers were still in it. Not until I got back to my table did I "crash" as I realized what I had just gone through. My friends took one look at my face and demanded to know what happened. I really didn't know exactly what had happened, but I gave them the details as I remembered them. They advised me not to bother summoning the police. Even if the men were found, nothing could be proven, and it would only lead to a long detention for us while dealing with the police.

When we left the restaurant, however, the two Russian men were standing across the street staring at the restaurant—probably wondering, like I was, what had happened. Instead of waiting for our bus to pick us up, we hailed a cab and returned to our hotel.

Over a period of a few years, I made about thirteen trips to the former Soviet Union, and nothing like that ever happened to me again. The Russian people were almost always eager to meet us and to interact with us. They were overwhelmingly grateful for the message we brought and the materials we left with them, and a large majority of them became believers during the course of the convocation they attended. Many of them became dear friends, with whom we still keep in touch. So I can't say my one experience at that Moscow restaurant was typical. It was as out of the ordinary as was my miraculous delivery, which had to be by God's hand. I have thought of that over the years and have tried to fill in the blanks, but I still have no idea how I got outside that restroom door. I only know that when I read, "Fear not, for I am with you," it has a whole new meaning for me. I have experienced God's deliverance firsthand.

12

A STORMY BLESSING

CAROL CHASE

I flopped onto a berth in our small sailboat, wiping my salt-burned eyelids and yearning for the cool of evening. For several days our yacht had been drifting aimlessly under the hot Pacific sun, 150 miles off the Mexican coast.

We need wind, Lord! Where is the wind? I asked for the hundredth time. We don't always know what we ask for.

My husband, Lyle, and I were on the final leg of a journey around the world. Twenty-five days earlier we had left the Republic of Panama hoping to sail nonstop to Canada. Instead of making good progress north, however, we found ourselves becalmed day after day, forced to use precious supplies far too soon in the journey.

We've gone two miles in two days, and there are still 3,400 miles to go, I griped mentally, as I again wiped perspiration from my sore eyes.

Lyle had been occupied in the cockpit when he suddenly called down into the cabin. "It looks like our water maker's broken."

Sore eyes forgotten, I bolted up into the cockpit, where Lyle was reassembling the unit after his attempt to repair it.

"I know what's wrong, but I can't fix it without the right

part," he sighed. If anyone could have worked around the problem, I knew Lyle could, so I just stared dumbly at him, trying to absorb the situation.

Our water maker converted salt water into fresh, not only supplementing our two small drinking water tanks but also providing water for showering each day, without which our skin would soon break down in the heat. The unit acted as an exercise machine, as well, because we had to pump it by hand. The water maker was brand new, and I was stunned at losing this vital piece of equipment.

"What do we do now?" I asked numbly. "We'll never make it home with just the water we have."

"We're going into Acapulco," Lyle said, managing to calm me. "There's a big marina there. We can order the part and get on our way again fast," he added confidently. We had carefully timed our journey to avoid any storms in the Pacific, and a long delay could endanger us. So, after making a few preparations, we started the engine and headed east toward Mexico.

Twenty-four hours later, we entered Acapulco Harbor, having devised the "perfect plan" to deal with this frustrating setback and continue our journey home as soon as possible. Step one of the plan was to find just the right place to moor our yacht. We scanned the beautiful, newly built marina in front of us.

"I see a good spot," Lyle said enthusiastically, pointing to one of the empty outer docks. "It's away from everything, peaceful, and it'll be easy to leave when we're ready. Hopefully, we'll be on our way again in a week."

"It looks like a heaven-sent blessing to me." I smiled back. We were weary from traveling all night and eager to get settled and rested up.

As Lyle steered toward the dock, step one of our "perfect plan" seemed to be succeeding—for about thirty seconds, that is—when from seemingly nowhere a lanky, smiling, arm-waving marina attendant appeared on a different dock and beckoned us to follow him.

"*Buenos días*," I called to him in my friendliest Spanish and pointed hopefully toward the vacant dock where we were heading. He shook his head, smiled even more broadly, and directed us instead to the inner heart of the busy marina.

"He's the boss." Lyle shrugged as we maneuvered past numerous luxury powerboats and steered farther in toward shore. The attendant's nonstop arm signals guided us steadily as he bounded from dock to dock until he finally stopped and pointed to the place where he wanted us to tie up. Our hearts sank.

No, no! Not there, please, I begged silently. The attendant had assigned us to the busiest spot in the marina, closest to shore, where the foot ramp led up to the marina offices. Privacy was impossible, and navigation could be tricky in certain conditions, as there was nothing between us and the rocks onshore. With a final, happy grin and a wave, the dock attendant danced off to attend to other matters, and we never saw him again.

Step two of our "perfect plan" disintegrated when we learned that the part we needed would take at least three weeks to arrive. The only option was to wait it out patiently. We were not particularly grateful for our assigned spot in the marina, but as the weeks passed, we learned to accept the constant flow of people past our vessel. We befriended other sailors around the docks and had long talks with the friendly marina staff, who loved to practice their English while we practiced our Spanish.

It was a Friday morning, three weeks later, when we learned our part had arrived. At last we could take step three of the now defunct "perfect plan"—pick up the part and resume our journey north.

By the time we had completed the necessary paperwork, however, and provisioned for the upcoming trip, it was late afternoon. A breeze had started, and a nasty chop was developing in the normally smooth harbor waters, so we decided to leave the following morning and let the weather settle down. Lyle went below to sleep while I stayed in the cockpit to read.

A sense of uneasiness suddenly began to intrude as the light breeze shifted into a stronger wind and the choppy waters beat against the shore. I noticed some of the boats at anchor were changing location in the harbor, but there was no real protection anywhere.

The motion inside our yacht and the straining of the lines awakened Lyle. He stuck his head out of the hatch sleepily and asked, "What's going on?"

"I think you'd better get dressed. The wind's up, and we'll probably be on watch all night," I replied tensely.

As the hours passed, conditions deteriorated, and it became evident we were in a full-scale hurricane. There had been no previous warning. People were yelling on the docks, and we watched, horrified, as several large powerboats broke loose and were driven past us onto the rocks, only to be smashed into unrecognizable pieces.

Marina workers and boat owners alike risked their lives trying to salvage vessels as entire docks broke apart and floated away, producing dangerous debris in the water. We constantly adjusted our mooring lines to ease the strain and started our engine, putting it into reverse to help keep us off the rocks just a few yards in front of us.

Please, God, help us all, I prayed over and over.

It was still dark, and we were thirteen hours into the storm when Lyle and I finally accepted that we had to abandon ship and seek shelter in the marina building ashore. We were the last yacht to do so. Soon we wouldn't be able to get safely ashore as our dock, also, had started to break up and we could see the violence of the water through the holes left by several missing planks. We assembled passports, money, and a few personal items; then we went ashore to join a large group of exhausted men and women sitting or sleeping on the carpeted floor of the marina building.

As we waited for the hurricane to pass, I grieved everyone's losses that had occurred in the past few hours and tried not to think of the destruction of our own yacht, which had been our only home for the past fifteen years.

With the coming of daybreak, the hurricane finally passed and shouts of relief could be heard everywhere. People got up from the floor and went outside to assess the damage in the light of day. Lyle and I moved slowly to the door, dreading what awaited us.

To our shock, the first thing we saw was our sailboat—undamaged, with the engine still running—and the dock still firmly intact, albeit with a few planks missing.

"It's still there!" I cried. Lyle and I hugged each other tightly and wept tears of stunned relief.

Looking farther out at the debris and devastation that had been a beautiful marina less than twenty-four hours previously, we could see that the dock to which we had been so eager to tie, when we first entered the harbor, no longer existed. It had simply broken away and disappeared into the night, to be dashed to pieces somewhere on the shore. Furthermore, we were the only vessel to suffer no damage other than a little loss of paint where lines had chafed.

Over and over again, words tumbled through my mind. *Thank You, Lord, for saving our yacht! Thank You for the attendant You sent to guide us to THIS exact spot. Thank You for the enduring dock and strong lines! You knew exactly where we needed to be to survive the storm unharmed!*

It was another six days before we could finally leave Acapulco safely with our repaired water maker, but we left with a heightened appreciation for life, for friends, and for the marina workers who had risked their safety to help with rescue efforts.

Most of all, we left with a profound spiritual gratitude. We knew the divine protection we received was extraordinary—never to be taken for granted, but rather acknowledged as a special grace from a merciful God, to be cherished in our hearts for the rest of our lives.

13

GLAD TO BE ALIVE

SUZETTE PRUIT

"This has been a most memorable vacation," I had written my parents only the night before. "I feel as if I've come closer to understanding myself and my place in the world."

Now I lay awake on a hospital cot, tossing and turning but happy to be able to toss and turn. My great-aunt lay in a bed a few feet from me, and her occasional moans revealed her pain.

I had come to visit my father's seventy-year-old aunt in Richmond, Virginia, hoping to learn more about his side of the family. His parents had died before I was born, and the only relative of his whom I had met was his only brother, who died suddenly when I was in eighth grade. This aunt, the youngest in a large family in my father's home state of Virginia, many miles from our Michigan home, was the last of her generation. While we had written each other through the years, we had never met.

My two weeks at Aunt Grace's home were magical. She filled me with stories of the family and introduced me to cousins. She also drove me around the city, which was beautiful and dense with history. I was grateful for her doing this; however, I found her poor driving skills somewhat unsettling.

On my last full day of vacation, we toured historic Williamsburg, and I was full to the brim with pride and joy—as an American, as a member of a loving family, as a young adult with a life of possibility ahead of me.

"Are you tired, Aunt Grace?" I asked as we got in the car for the ride home. It was dark; our last activity in Williamsburg had been an outdoor show with fireworks at dusk. "If you are, I can drive." My suggestion was as much out of uneasiness about her driving in the dark as it was out of kindness.

"Thank you, dear," she said. "I may let you if I find I'm getting drowsy. But I feel quite wide awake, and it's only an hour's drive or so. Just talk to me, and I'll be all right."

That was easy for me to do, and we seemed safe enough. It was a little past 11 p.m., and the highway was practically deserted. As I talked, though, I was aware that a flashing light was ahead, alerting drivers to make a four-way stop at the junction of another highway, and I realized, too late, that Aunt Grace did not see it and that she was not going to stop.

To my right I could see a pair of headlights coming straight at our car. There was no time to shout, no time to scream. Instinctively, I thought, *It's up to You, Jesus*, and I relaxed, waiting for it to be over. What happened next was a loud noise, then a whirling that felt not unlike an amusement park ride.

I had no sensation of being hit or having fallen. When the whirling stopped, I was lying on soft grass with something on my back. *The car is on top of me*, I thought, but as I moved my arm, I saw it was a sign relating gasoline prices. Our car had uprooted it from the gas station lawn we had landed on.

I sat up, felt my arms and legs, knew I was still in one piece, and I whispered, "Thank You, Jesus."

My thoughts then sprang to my great-aunt. "Aunt Grace!" I called. I saw her lying on the grass near me, and I reached out to her. "Are you all right?" I said. No sound came. The fear that had escaped me during the crash hit. Tearful, I cried out, "Aunt Grace! Are you all right? Please be all right! Please, please, Aunt Grace!"

She stirred and gave me a bewildered look. "What happened?" she murmured.

"We were hit, Aunt Grace, but we're all right."

"Are you all right?" she asked me, trying to raise herself.

"Yes, I'm fine. Better lie still till you're sure you're okay," I said, patting her gently on the arm.

We were joined by several people who seemed to come out of nowhere. Here we were in a tiny community at a little before midnight, yet several people had gathered around us, and they were trying to help. Someone was dabbing at my shoulder with a handkerchief, but I said, "Don't worry about me. It's only a little cut. Just see that she's all right."

"What happened?" Aunt Grace said again. She had never seen the car that hit us, I realized. I wondered which of us had known the greater shock, I who had been prepared for the blow—as much as anyone could be prepared—or my great-aunt, who had not even known it was coming.

The car was a few feet from us, and I got up to take a look at it. We had been hit on my side of the car, a few inches from the door. The blow had been sufficient to buckle the backseat.

The passenger door was closed tight, and the driver's side was open, so it was obvious that we had both fallen out the driver's side. Aunt Grace had probably cushioned my fall.

The other car was damaged in its front end, but the driver seemed to be unhurt.

An ambulance arrived, soon after the uniformed officers and "good Samaritans." The paramedics loaded Aunt Grace into the ambulance as I walked around the lawn, picking up items thrown from our car. I picked up her purse and its spilled contents, my bag, and even some used tissue. I also tried to pick up the stump from the gas station sign (a sure indication that I was in a bit of shock myself). I then climbed in the ambulance with Aunt Grace.

"What happened, dear? Are you all right?" Aunt Grace kept asking me in the ride to the hospital. Though I answered, she would ask the same question again, over and over.

The doctor examined Aunt Grace in the emergency room first, and then he came to me in a smaller room. He told me that she had broken ribs and that she would have complete X-rays and further treatment in the morning.

"And now, what about you, young lady?" the doctor said to me.

"I'm beginning to feel some pain around my middle," I said. He examined my midriff but found nothing awry.

"You must have slid past the steering wheel," he said. "That would explain the discomfort." He smiled and patted my shoulder. "I can promise you plenty of aches and big, colorful bruises in the next few days. You may be most uncomfortable, but from what I understand of the accident, you were mighty lucky."

The sheriff's deputy, who questioned me about the accident later, seconded the doctor's opinion. "If that car had hit you two inches from the spot it did, you wouldn't be here talking to me tonight," he said.

The hospital staff brought in a cot for me so that I could share Aunt Grace's hospital room for the night. A young nurse, Miss Finch, took me to the room.

"I had an accident a couple of years ago," Miss Finch said softly as we walked down the hall. "Mine was a bad one, too, but I wasn't hurt. It got me to thinking. I had a strange feeling that maybe I was 'spared' for a greater purpose. At a time like that, no one can help you, and it's just between you and God. I felt that He was with me that night."

"I felt Him tonight," I said. I was glad to talk about that with someone. "I've gone to church and said I believed in Him; I've gone through periods of faith and periods of being 'impatient' with God; I've prayed to Him and tried to understand His will for me. But God was never so real to me as He was tonight. I felt His presence very strongly."

We were at the door of Aunt Grace's hospital room. "And what will you do now?" Miss Finch whispered.

"Try to keep Him from regretting His faith in me, I guess," I said.

I lay awake much of the night, partly because of Aunt Grace's soft groans as the nurses checked on her, but also because my active mind kept going over the accident, thinking of my vacation up to that point, and pondering my whole purpose in life. I had been enjoying my first job after college, but I knew I was not where I should stay. I needed to move on. That would mean leaving the comforts of home, making new friends and alliances, having the courage to pursue employment that would use the skills God had given me.

It would also mean finding a new church, one that would help me in my now-stronger desire to fulfill the mission God had for me. I had been blessed with the family, the friends, the church, and the job I had, but God had more for me to do. I had been somewhat fearful of going into the unknown, but what I had learned in this vacation made me understand that God would provide, no matter where I was.

In the morning, as I got ready for my cousins to pick me up to take me to the train station, I said good-bye to my great-aunt, who was already feeling better (or at least well enough to be her polite self). "It was wonderful having you here," she told me.

"I had a lovely vacation," I told Aunt Grace. "I learned so much this summer."

14

GOD'S PROTECTION

DEEDRE MARTZ

And even the very hairs of your head are all numbered.
So don't be afraid; you are worth more than many sparrows.

MATTHEW 10:30-31 NIV

"Hey, look at that snow. It's coming down fast," said Colleen, as I passed her in the hall. As we rushed through the corridor, we both caught a glance through the window of giant snowflakes covering the tall evergreens. "It looks like we'll be closing early today."

What a wonderful gift to start the holiday. It gave us all a little extra time off from our busy office, and we were all exhausted. However, I was dreading the knuckle-clenched, stiff-shoulder drive through the snowstorm that I'd have to endure to make it home.

"Dee, do you have your bus schedule with you?" asked Laura. I knew her tires were bald, and that she had no heater in her little red Volkswagen Rabbit.

"Do you want a ride instead?"

"Thanks. That would be great."

We walked to the parking lot. The snow was coming

down fast and had already covered the cars and pavement with nearly a foot. We brushed the snow off my SUV and started the undoubtedly slow-going journey to our homes. All was well until we came to the edge of the city where all the roads led uphill. The first route we tried had a long line of cars. After about a half hour, I doubled back to a more northern road with less traffic, and we actually cruised at about 20 mph.

We continued moving forward at this pace until an oncoming car at a curve in the road caused us to slide into a ditch, narrowly missing two cars that were already stuck there.

"Oh great. Now we have to figure out how to get out of this ditch," I said with disgust.

"Aren't we fortunate to have our office Christmas gifts of food and candles in case we're stuck here awhile?" said Laura, adding sarcasm and levity to the situation.

"And there are matches in the glove box and a blanket in here, too," I added. One of the advantages that comes with age is that you're prepared for survival.

Believing we were stronger than we actually were, we tried pushing the front of the car. After watching the pathetic attempts made by us middle-aged women, the young men in one of the other stuck cars got out and tried to help us. In doing so, my car slid behind theirs, so now they weren't going anywhere without our car moving first.

I tried digging the snow out from around the front wheel and was squatting to look at my progress.

"LOOK OUT!" yelled Laura, as a sliding car missed my head by inches and crunched my bumper instead.

What! I was almost struck in the head by a car? I realized the gravity of what just about happened as my heart felt like it was going to burst through my chest. God spared my life—it was a wakeup call.

. . . .

Five months later, during a Friday night rush hour, my husband and I stopped at the bank. Paul was standing at the drive-up ATM, and I was sitting in the driver's seat when a bloody-faced man appeared at my passenger-side window.

"Hey, can you give me a ride to a mechanic? I'll give you twenty dollars. My car broke down. I need to get to a mechanic."

He had blood on his forehead and mouth, and what looked like a few teeth knocked out. I thought he'd been injured in a fight and was intoxicated, but not dangerous.

He kept repeating his request. "Can you give me a ride to my mechanic? I'll give you twenty dollars."

I don't ever give strangers rides, so pointing to the business next door, I said, "There's a gas station right there. Maybe they can help you and would have a phone."

He then went to Paul, who was focused on making his transaction at the ATM. Paul didn't notice the man's appearance and said, "I'm doing a transaction right now, just a minute." Then...

"POLICE! PUT YOUR HANDS UP AND DROP YOUR WEAPON!" shouted one of a half dozen officers with guns pointed at the man—and us. I felt like I was watching a movie scene, instead of a live event with me in it. The man moved in front of where I was sitting in the driver's seat. If the police fired, they would shoot him, then I would be in the line of fire through the windshield. Still feeling that none of this was really happening, I jumped out of the car and ran to the side of the bank, out of the way.

Paul, at this point, as surprised as I was with this unlikely crime-scene drama, went to where I was standing, out of harm's way.

Then the man, demonstrating genuine criminal insanity, got into my car, as if he could steal it in front of a half dozen police officers with guns aimed at him.

"My car keys?" I said. They were in my hand. "Thank You, Lord."

The policemen took the man from my car, cuffed him, and began questioning him.

Still in disbelief, I watched quietly. It took me a while to start shaking and realize what had actually taken place because in my mind these situations just don't happen here. I live in a low crime city with good schools—a number-one city in America to live in, according to *Money* magazine.

The officers told us the man had tried to rob the grocery store, stole a car, smashed it into the side of the building across the street, then walked from that car to us. The blood on his face was from injuries from that accident. He was also reported to have had a gun that he'd thrown into a nearby field.

If we had seen the cops assembling behind the bushes, we

would have panicked. But we were unaware and, therefore, amazingly calm, taking our time, acting like nothing was unusual. I feel God was intervening behind the scenes by having us not react, which perfectly orchestrated the timing for the police to position for the arrest.

Coming close to death is about as scary as it gets. My story isn't monumental, like surviving a war zone or tornado, but through these personal experiences in my own everyday life, God revealed to me that He is real and near. I know I will have trials and one day will die, but knowing God cares for me, one of the little sparrows, gives me comfort I will count on the rest of my life.

PART 3

GOD'S
HEALING

15

THREES

DAVID MICHAEL SMITH

They say things run in threes. This is a true story about a man who cried three times over his children. This is a roller-coaster ride complete with summits and valleys of mixed, raw emotions, days of darkness and redeeming light at the end of cavernous tunnels. This is a story about my family and me.

The first time I cried I was actually childless, but it wasn't for a lack of trying. My wife, Geralynn, and I had been married for seven years and since our honeymoon had tried to start a family. After a year or so of failed attempts, we began to reach out for help to expedite matters, beginning a parade of countless and sometimes embarrassing visits to doctors, urologists, gynecologists, and eventually fertility experts and clinics. Each member of the medical community probed and prodded and examined us like rats in a lab. We utilized every methodology known, every tip or hint or trick family members could propose, even the outrageous, as well as ovulation kits and the more conventional options in our journey to get pregnant. We participated in artificial insemination procedures and several rounds of in vitro fertilization. Family, friends, and congregations prayed for us. Nothing worked.

With each letdown, where you get yourself sky high but then come crashing back down to earth with a thud, our emotions became like frayed ropes or splintered wood. We were tired, sad, and disappointed but mostly empty. A big hole of barrenness existed in our lives, and we wished to the stars that it could be filled with a chubby-cheeked, cooing baby.

Then it happened, actually on our own, which made it doubly exciting: my wife announced that she was pregnant! Every day was like Christmas Eve for a couple of weeks, and it was hard not to rejoice and share the good news. We tried to remain optimistic, yet cautious, taking life one day at a time. My wife did everything right, and she was the model pregnant woman. Her face shined with joy. Life, a little baby, *our* baby, was growing in her womb.

But then our worst fears were realized one morning when my wife began to bleed while showering. We went directly to the doctor's office, praying to God for His intervention and healing grace. Geri was thoroughly examined, blood drawn, and tests run. We would know more the following day.

That night neither of us could sleep. We continued to pray for a miracle, *our* miracle child to be saved. The following day I was off from work, but my wife went to the office as planned. She kissed me good-bye, and we both silently hoped for good news. That afternoon the phone rang, and a kindly nurse delivered in the best way possible very grave news: my wife had miscarried and the pregnancy had arrested. I was devastated and could barely speak, but I worried more about my wife's reaction.

An hour later my wife came home. I was already outside and nervously approached the car. I just wanted to fast-forward our lives to a better, happier day. She tentatively exited her car and our eyes met.

She managed, "Did you hear . . . ?"

But she already knew the answer, as my lips quivered to answer but instead I began to sob uncontrollably. We held each other for what seemed hours, cried lakes of tears, and prayed, each time asking God to take good care of our child. Knowing our baby was in heaven gave us comfort, but we existed with a great loneliness for many months to come.

This was the first time I cried over my child, one lost before we ever met, and now a citizen of Paradise.

After I turned forty-four, I told my wife that after nine failed years of trying to have a baby, the writing, for me at least, was on the wall. We would never experience the joys and challenges of parenthood, and I would never hold a child that I could call my own. I would always be an uncle or a godparent, maybe a "big brother," but not a daddy. And that hurt.

We'd discussed adoption a few times during the years, but it seemed when it was plausible for my wife, I wasn't sure of my interest. And when I warmed up to the idea, my wife became unsure of her feelings. One thing we both agreed upon, and that was it would be wrong to adopt a child if both of us weren't fully committed to it.

Then, driving home from work one evening together we looked at each other simultaneously and began to speak the same sentence. "You know, I think maybe adoption might just be a great idea after all!" Something within each of us had cleared any roadblocks of apprehension or indecision. And with renewed energy and excitement, and a spirit of dedication, it was at that very moment we decided to adopt.

We researched the various programs available, and there were many. Eventually we decided, after exhaustive, thorough efforts, to adopt a little girl from China due to the country's cruel and inhumane treatment of their children, specifically baby girls. It took nearly a year and a half of assembling paperwork, fingerprinting, and jumping through a variety of international and domestic legal hoops, but during Memorial Day weekend in late May of 2004 we jetted to China, a fifteen-hour flight from start to finish. After two days of sightseeing in Beijing, we flew south to Guangzhou and within hours were escorted into a hot, humid government room with other nervous but excited parents-to-be. Minutes later several nannies from the orphanage, which we were not allowed to visit during our stay, entered the room, each holding bundled, frightened infant girls. We had already chosen our daughter's name and seen photos of her; Rebekah Joy Ji Smith was nearly eleven months old at the time. Everything about her was picture perfect.

Several names were called before us, but then the moment arrived. I thought my heart would stop beating, and tiny beads of perspiration sluiced down my cheeks.

"Smith? Smith?"

My wife stepped forward slowly as I captured the memory forever on a camcorder. Our daughter was handed to us, and she was the only baby not to cry. She gazed up at my wife, then me, and everyone fell in love at once. We were a family, a radiantly happy and blessed family.

And when I held her that day I cried for the second time, for this was my daughter, a gift from heaven.

After returning to the states we were content. It had taken nearly a decade, but our family was now complete. But God had a surprise for us, an absolute, undeniable miracle! Only a few months after returning home with Rebekah in tow, Geri became pregnant, very pregnant, and healthily pregnant! Ironically, one Sunday prior to our traveling to China, this very event was prophesied in our church by our bishop, Richard Lipka. When the prophecy came to fruition, we were stunned. In the past, medical professionals had told us point-blank that we simply would never get pregnant without scientific assistance due to bad egg quality and endometriosis. But here we were, pregnant nonetheless, and this time everything worked out perfectly.

Nearly nine months later, my wife's water broke very early one morning and off to the hospital we went, apprehensive but mostly joyous. As it would turn out, though, labor would be hard and long for my wife, and when day became night and night became the next morning, the doctor ordered a Cesarean section. We were both exhausted. Neither of us had slept a wink, and any excitement we had felt early on in the process had long expired. My wife just wanted the baby out!

They initially left me in the hallway alone with my thoughts outside of the operating room, dressed in a blue mask and hospital scrubs, as they prepped my wife inside. Later they allowed me inside as the doctor began the surgery. As each second passed, my anticipation mounted to the point where I thought I was going to implode. I wanted to see my son, hold him, kiss his face, and tell him I loved him.

Finally the doctor extracted my son from the womb and held him up so we could see him, and then he handed the child off to a quartet of nurses who immediately went to work cleaning him up and ensuring he was breathing properly. But at that moment when my son was aloft, despite being covered in mucus and blood and other fluids, my heart burst with joy. Only two other sights were of equal beauty: the day my wife glided gracefully down the aisle when we were wed in church and the day I was handed my daughter overseas. Our son, Matthew Robert Smith, was absolutely beautiful to me. I wanted to rush over to him and kiss and cuddle him. Silently I praised God, who is always good.

Minutes later we were united, exhausted mother, proud father, and newborn son. And for the third time I cried.

16

A MIDNIGHT RIDE FOR HELP

PATRICIA STEBELTON

It was November in 1965. I stared anxiously out the front window into the blackness of the country terrain. On this late Sunday evening there was no moon, but I could see frantic tree limbs gyrating in the wind. We were housebound—prisoners inside our home—and I'd become increasingly distressed over the unrelenting rain, accompanied by a pressing feeling I couldn't identify. Everything pointed to it being a uneventful night, and yet I couldn't shake my inner restlessness and I continued to search the darkness outside for relief of my uneasy spirit. Hopefully, I would see a sign that the rain was diminishing? If the rain stopped now, perhaps everything would be all right . . . .

Only recently had our dream been realized. We lived a good five miles from a charming small town, surrounded by rolling hills and twisting two-lane country roads. Moving out from the city, we thought we'd found the perfect living situation, never realizing there would be drawbacks in our choice—especially during critical situations. The hospital was twenty miles away.

A few weeks prior we had moved into our country home, and our minds were filled with excited plans for our young family. We had much work to do, but here we were, trapped inside by the weather. It was essential for a solid driveway to be established before winter, then next a lawn to keep the raw topsoil from eroding. Time was short! It was already late fall; winter was rushing to take its place.

I bit my lip. *Would this rain never stop?* For days now there had been no letup, and our new home sat as an island in a virtual lake of mud. It required our cars to be parked across the road at our nearest neighbor's place—four hundred feet from the county road. My husband's parents had left earlier, taking our four-year-old daughter home for a visit. After riding herd most of the day on our energetic, eighteen-month-old son, Michael, it took multiple tries to put him to bed. We heaved a sigh of relief when he finally settled down for the night.

For two hours now the house had been quiet, but I was still unable to relax. Feeling coldness seep through the glass, I rubbed my arms. The temperature was dropping fast, turning rain into sleet. Seeing it pelt the windows, my frustration grew. *At this rate, we'll never get a driveway in!* As I turned from the window to join my husband, Dick, I heard a startling sound.

It was unlike anything I'd ever heard before. A paralyzing chill shot down my spine. Exchanging fearful glances with Dick, I tore to the nursery with my husband. Our son's face was dark red as he strained to breathe, creating a deep, barking sound—not quite human in tone. My chest filled with terror. I caressed his face. Michael was burning up with fever!

My husband held him while I frantically dialed the doctors' office. The fact that it was Sunday night, almost eleven o'clock, didn't register until an answering service gave its rote message. "The office is closed until Monday . . . if this is an emergency, go to St. Joseph's Hospital, Ann Arbor." *So far away, Lord!* My mind panicked. I sensed Michael's condition was critical. We had no choice!

Barely taking time to grab a jacket, Dick pulled on his boots and raced out into the night. He raced through the driving rain two hundred feet to the county road, then four hundred feet up the neighbor's drive. I pulled on my raincoat and boots, worried how I could carry our flailing son across that dark, muddy terrain to meet Dick at the road. It was so dark!

Every uncertain step I took, my boots sucked further into the mud, draining my strength with each effort to move. I pulled the blanket around Michael and tried to shield my baby from the cold sheets of water pounding us without mercy. "God!" I cried into the wind. "Can't You stop this rain until we get to the hospital? Our baby can't breathe!" Afraid that the chilled, wet weather would surely make him worse, I didn't understand why God wouldn't answer my prayer. He'd answered so many before. *Where is He now?*

"Save my baby, Jesus." Visions of childhood tormented my thoughts. My baby brother had died when he was the same age as our son. I fought the rising fear within me. Dick was waiting for me on the road, but our progress was slow. "Can't you drive faster?" I demanded accusingly.

"I can't see through the windshield! If we get in a wreck, we'll never get to the hospital!" he retorted, his voice strained with worry.

I knew he was right, but I couldn't tolerate the lengthy time it was taking to get our baby help. Time and the infuriating rain were our enemies. Rocking Michael, I murmured soothing words and prayed unceasingly, trying to keep faith that everything would be all right—but even the car heater was reluctant to aid our discomfort. The cold, outside dampness permeated the car. I gripped my watch, realizing it would be nearly midnight by the time we arrived and groaned inwardly at the forced delay. Watching Michael laboring to breathe was strangling my heart. Would we be too late? Would another child die before Christmas?

Reaching the city limits, it took forever to wait at long lights and weave our way through narrow side streets. They took Michael from us in the emergency room of St. Joseph's Hospital, and we waited anxiously for a report. After long minutes, a solemn hospital resident talked to us in low tones. Michael had been admitted to the hospital and was currently being taken to his room. There was more news, and it wasn't good. Our baby might have to have an emergency tracheotomy before the night was over.

The resident tried to explain, "In cases of 'croup' in children under the age of two, this is always a grave possibility." Dick and I found hope in the blessing that the foremost specialist in this type of surgery *just happened* to be in the hospital at this time. He promised to remain until the crisis was past. The long wait began, and we paced the small room.

After midnight, the dark silence of the hospital corridors had an unnerving effect on our rising apprehension. Finally summoned upstairs, we spoke in hushed whispers as we rode the empty elevator and stepped softly out on the children's floor, hurrying toward our son's room. The lighting was dim as we rushed inside. My hand flew to my mouth, alarmed at the sight. Michael was enclosed within a plastic tent secured tight about his crib.

Seeing me, he began to cry and lifted his arms to be held. I ached to take him and comfort his confusion. When I looked to the nurse, she shook her head. It was important that he remain inside the tent, which I took to be filled with oxygen. Dick and I sat close to Michael's bed and waited until our baby calmed. Every limb of our bodies was weary with stress and anxiety . . . and the minutes ticked slowly by.

It was almost two hours before the doctor made his decision that surgery would not be necessary. Immediately a huge weight lifted from our shoulders, and our eyes flooded with tears of relief. Approaching the nurse, I begged to stay through the night with our child, but hospital policy wouldn't allow it. "How long will he have to be in that oxygen tent?" I asked.

"That's not oxygen. He's in a cold steam tent. It's the best thing for children with croup. He'll probably need to remain here a few days, but it will depend on his progress," she answered.

I stared at her in shock, then back at the billowing plastic tent. "Cold steam—really?"

The nurse nodded with assurance. "The cold steam will also assist with bringing down his temperature. Being in that tent will help him the most at this time."

It took a few minutes for me to process her information. As Dick and I walked the hallway toward the elevator, we heard Michael's hoarse cry, calling for us. It was so hard to leave him there, but I knew he was safe, getting the help he needed. What I couldn't get over, however, was the fact that all the time I inwardly cursed the cold, unrelenting rain, our Lord had surrounded our baby in cold steam—saving him. Even the specialty doctor we'd need was on hand to help us on a Sunday at midnight. What I thought was our enemy had been a blessing in disguise. God had been with us through the mud and the sleet. He had placed us safely in the eye of the storm and provided our shelter, and we were truly blessed.

17

HE WAS THERE

BONNIE LEON

My four-year-old daughter, Kristi, snuggled close while I read a *Winnie the Pooh* story to her. All of a sudden, she covered the page with her hand and looked up at me. I brushed a soft, blond curl off her face. "What is it, Kristi?"

"Mommy, I had a dream." Seeming to ponder what to say next, she stared down at her hands. "It was a long, long time ago. In my dream I was dying. I was so scared."

My throat tightened, and memories of a frantic trip to the hospital three and a half years before filled my thoughts. I knew this was not a dream, but a little girl's memory.

That day had started like any other, but by late afternoon my eight-month-old's early morning crankiness had shifted to a full-fledged tirade. She was running a mild fever, but I was convinced it was nothing more than teething and so I lay her down for a nap.

A short forty-five minutes later, Kristi's moaning and whimpering drew me to her crib. She thrashed at the bedding, and when I picked her up I knew right away that she was very sick. Heat radiated through her clothing, and her breathing was shallow and rapid.

I took her temperature—105 degrees!

My reaction was not what I would have expected. I panicked. *Lord, help us,* I prayed as I called my husband at work. When he answered, I choked back a sob. "Greg, we've got to get Kristi to the hospital! She's really sick!"

I'd never felt such fear for one of my children. For reasons I didn't understand then, this time was different.

"Calm down," I told myself. "It's just a fever. Kristi's had fevers before." No matter how reasonable I tried to sound, my anxiety wouldn't be quieted.

While I waited for my husband, the air felt heavy with dread. Holding my daughter close, I paced the room, moving from window to window, hoping to see his car.

When he pulled into the driveway, I hurried out to meet him. Clutching Kristi to my chest, I slid onto the seat beside him. "We've got to hurry!"

We headed toward town, twenty miles away. I wanted to believe Kristi was going to be fine, but as the green hills flashed by, fear pierced my heart. *Lord,* I pleaded, *I've always believed You would protect my children. I can't bear to lose my baby. Please help her.*

The emergency room was packed with sick and injured. We waited our turn, and when we finally saw the doctor, he was pressed for time and made a hurried diagnosis. "She has a sinus infection," he said. "We'll get her on an antibiotic, and she should feel better by tomorrow."

Greg and I returned home, relieved and a little embarrassed by our unreasonable alarm. But as the hours passed Kristi seemed to get worse, and my apprehension returned.

Could the doctor have been wrong?

Throughout the night, Kristi moaned and whimpered. She seemed extremely ill, but I trusted the doctor. When her temperature dropped, I whispered a prayer of thanks. I didn't recognize that her cold, clammy skin signaled a decline in her condition. She was in shock and I had no idea.

When I tried to hold her, she whimpered and pushed against me as if my touch was painful to her. I could find no way to comfort her. It was a long night filled with tears and prayers. My husband and I were not the only ones praying. I discovered later that a friend had been awakened repeatedly during the night with an urgency to pray for our daughter. I am grateful for her compliant heart.

By morning, Kristi was quiet, unwilling to drink, and her eyes were open but unresponsive. Her cries had become pitiful and monotone.

As daylight stretched its cool fingers across my living room floor, I roused my husband and we set off for our pediatrician's office. The nurse peeked at Kristi, and her face blanched. She took my daughter from me and hurried to the back offices in search of the doctor.

Greg and I followed, knowing something was terribly wrong.

The doctor examined Kristi and then turned to us, his expression somber. He placed a hand on my shoulder. "Kristi has an infection of the central nervous system—spinal meningitis."

My legs went weak, and my heart pounded erratically. I

reached for my husband's hand and held on tight while the doctor explained Kristi was in critical condition and needed to be hospitalized.

We rushed to the hospital, where we were met at the entrance by a nurse. We stepped inside and the odor of disinfectants burned my nose. The nurse took Kristi from me, and as she walked away I wondered if I'd ever see my little girl alive again.

Greg and I filled out paperwork then waited in stiff-backed chairs, feeling invisible amid the impersonal, antiseptic world of the hospital.

After performing a spinal tap on Kristi, the doctor's prognosis was confirmed—spinal meningitis. It would take a few days for the tests to reveal which strain—Haemophilus.

Kristi was comatose, in shock, and septicemic. She was treated with powerful antibiotics and other lifesaving procedures. I stood outside the viewing window of her room, the doctor's words echoing through my mind. "*If* she's still alive after seventy-two hours, she *might* make it. Right now . . . she's crashing and burning."

Kristi was so tiny and helpless. Her hands were tied to the slats of a metal crib. Tubes protruded from her body, and the muscles in her neck had pulled her head so far backward that it lay against her back. I could hear her pitiable effort to cry and longed to hold her, to comfort her.

A nurse stood beside me and rested a hand on my arm. "She can't feel anything," she said kindly.

Tears came and sobs choked me. I had to get away. I ran

down the corridor, pushed through the doors at the end of the hall, and stumbled into a deserted playroom. Deep sobs wrenched themselves from me. Pain, unlike any I'd ever known, pierced my heart.

"God, this is too much! I can't bear it! Please save my little girl."

Quietly my husband came up behind me and pulled me into his arms. I felt his strength. For a long while we held each other, without sharing a word, and then Greg said, "I know she's going to be all right. God loves her. He'll take care of her."

Leaning on each other, we returned to Kristi's room. After donning gowns and masks, we went to her side, caressed her tiny hands, and asked God to touch our baby with His healing power. We also released her to His care.

Peace, beyond my ability to understand, replaced my fear. I knew God would do what was best. He was faithful.

Kristi made it through that first day and night and the next. When we arrived at the hospital the third morning, Kristi's nurse greeted us with a big smile. "She's awake!"

Joy bubbled up inside me, and I ran to her room.

I was finally allowed to hold Kristi, something I feared might never happen. I sat in a wooden rocker, and, amid a tangle of tubes, the nurse gently placed my little girl in my arms. The sickly sweet odor of antibiotics assaulted my senses, but all I cared about was that my daughter was alive and nestled against me.

Convinced Kristi would live, death was taken off the list

of possibilities, but there was another list, side effects—blindness, paralysis, cerebral palsy, epilepsy, mental retardation, hydrocephalus, and others.

In the days that followed, we watched and waited, seeking further signs of recovery—a smile, recognition in her eyes, a response to sound.

Doctors discovered Kristi was unable to use her left leg, and there was weakness on her left side as well as lack of coordination. They suspected cerebral palsy, so a CT scan was schedule then postponed when she improved. Then postponed again, and finally it was decided the test was unnecessary because Kristi was doing so well.

Fourteen days after being admitted, Kristi left the hospital. We were going home—together.

Kristi tugged on my sleeve and smiled up at me. "Jesus came and hugged me," she said, referring to her dream. "He held me on his lap, and I wasn't afraid anymore."

I looked down at my four-year-old bundle of energy and thanked God for her and for a Savior who always has time to hold His children. We didn't see Him there with her . . . but He'd been there.

18

BLESSINGS FOR THIS TIME AND PLACE

JANE OWEN

"Here's what we've been waiting for, Jane!" My husband, Ron, came from our mailbox waving an envelope over his head. He hurriedly opened it, and we stared at the announcement of our daughter Leah's upcoming graduation from the University of Utah's medical school. We looked at one another with pride, knowing the long road of study she had traveled.

Twelve years had passed, but I could still hear her request as an undergraduate—

"Mom, I'm thinking of pursuing a premed degree. Would you and Dad pray with me to know if this is what I should do?" Now, on May 22, 2010, she would enjoy the culmination of those years, earning her doctorate of medicine.

We arrived in Salt Lake City a couple of days prior to the anticipated event and were caught up in the festive preparations. That first evening Ron said, "My stomach hurts. Pray with me because I don't want to spoil this special time for Leah." He pressed his lips together. "Maybe I've simply eaten too much today," he added.

Ron had experienced two similar episodes eight months before. Each of those times the situation resolved on its own.

Since he didn't complain of any pain the next day, I assumed everything was fine.

On the 22nd, we left early for the auditorium to get good seats for taking pictures of her walking across the stage. The first chords of *Pomp and Circumstance* sounded, and we scanned the medical graduates for Leah. I spotted her, and the flashbacks began. There she was, nine months old, taking her first steps; then, running through the sprinkler with her best friends. I could still hear her strong voice, singing in her middle school choir. I smiled thinking of her first driving lesson and remembered her looking beautiful as she left with her date for the high school prom.

How did those years pass so quickly? My throat tightened and tears welled up. Reaching for Ron's handkerchief, I saw his eyes were misty, too.

After the ceremony, we gathered at Leah and her husband Tim's home. It was exhilarating to celebrate her achievement with family and friends, but I noticed Ron was quieter than usual. When he told me he needed to go back to our son's home to lie down, I was concerned. "Are you having more pain?" I asked.

"Yes, but I'll lie down and rest a while. Don't worry. If I need anything, I'll call you."

That evening, when I returned to the home of our son, Aaron, and his wife, Lindsey, I found Ron in excruciating discomfort. "I'm calling Leah," I said.

"No, Jane. Let's wait and see," he insisted. "It may pass, keep praying."

An hour went by, and another. The pain eased for short periods of time but did not cease completely. At one point, he bolted for the bathroom and vomited. Once more I suggested calling Leah. "I'm feeling better," he said. "If my system isn't settled by morning, I'll have her take me to the emergency room."

Ron fell asleep, and I called friends in Ohio to pray. The pain persisted, coming in waves. As those long night hours passed, I called others—our pastor in West Virginia, another good friend in Atlanta, and some folks there in Salt Lake City. I knew they would intercede and with us believe the Lord for the help Ron needed. The peace of God flowed into our situation at that moment. "Thank You, Father, for the blessing of Your ever-present care," I prayed. "Bless You for the faithfulness of these dear friends who stand with us for Ron's recovery." Then, I was able to fall asleep with that assurance from above. It was almost 5:00 a.m.

At 6:30 I awoke with a start. Ron was moaning. I grabbed the phone and called our daughter. Within minutes she and Tim arrived. She tenderly touched her dad's shoulder, assessing his condition, and we were on our way to the hospital. Because Leah recently had finished a rotation in the unit, she was able to facilitate Ron's care in the ER. To see the Lord synchronizing each detail brought tremendous peace to our hearts.

When we had a moment alone, I said, "Ron, God provided for you at this very time and place, long before it was this time and place."

He managed a slight smile. "Yes, and it's comforting to have Leah here with me," he said.

Again, I remembered the day Leah asked for prayer regarding her decision to study medicine—*Lord, the precision of Your provision for Ron's care is amazing!*

After several hours, Ron was admitted for an overnight stay in the hospital. The next morning, a CT scan revealed a blockage in the small intestine. A surgeon came to discuss the options. He explained that scar tissue from Ron's 1999 abdominal surgery for colon cancer had caused adhesions to grow and wrap around a section of bowel. "Sometimes these cases resolve on their own, but in your case, Ron, I believe we need to go in and 'unwrap' you."

We both wanted to know what was involved in "going in and unwrapping." The doctor said he hoped to perform the surgery laparoscopically. "Since the procedure is minimally invasive, I won't have to open you up," he explained. I called our brothers and sisters in Christ with these new details for prayer.

The following morning, before Ron went to surgery, Leah reassured us. "This surgeon is one of the very best laparoscopic surgeons in the western states. He is highly skilled." She smiled and patted her dad. "You are truly in good hands," she said as she left the room.

Ron was quiet for a moment, then gave me a wink. "I'm resting in God's hands, Jane," he whispered.

The actual removal of the adhesions took an hour and a half. Guided by the scope, the surgeon cut away each paper-thin tissue that bound the small bowel. When Ron was in the recovery room, one of the attending medical residents said, "It was amazing to watch each tiny piece of film snipped and removed. There were so many, we lost count."

I thanked God for a surgeon with a rock-steady hand who could perform such a delicate operation. The result was that Ron left the hospital three days later, fully recovered, with no limitations on his activities.

One of our dear friends in Salt Lake City summed up the results by saying, "I'm sure glad Ron came through like he did, but things always seem to work out right for him."

I smiled. "Things don't just work out for Ron," I gently replied. "The Lord's blessings aren't just for Ron. God hears anyone who prays and trusts in Him."

What a blessing to be at peace in the One who watches over our times and places! What an added blessing that our daughter, Leah, graduated from medical school one day, and the next morning, her dad was her first patient!

19

WHO CAN HELP ME?

SHIRLEY SHIBLEY

"Help me, help me!"

The voice was my husband's, but the words were garbled, and I wasn't sure I understood them correctly. I hurried into our bedroom, where Bob was trying to sleep away the symptoms of the "flu" or whatever. What I saw made me freeze in the doorway.

He was working his mouth like it wouldn't obey his directions. With the fingers of his right hand he pointed to his left arm. "I can't . . . I can't," his words stumbled out. His left arm lay as if paralyzed on the blanket.

The worst part was the fear in his eyes.

Fear gripped my own heart. Had Bob suffered a stroke? But he was only thirty-one! I finally jerked myself out of my frozen state and rushed to his side. I needed to help him but how? Fifty years ago our small town didn't have the advantage of calling 911 for emergency help. There was not even an emergency hospital, as there was in the larger city I grew up in. The best our town could offer was one doctor who traded with others in the medical office complex to act as emergency doctor. But I had to get Bob up and drive him there.

I helped him out of bed and to struggle into his bathrobe.

I put his feet into his slippers and explained I was going to take him to get help. Leaning on me with his good arm, he limped across the bedroom and to the front door. Getting him down the porch steps and into the car was a trial, but we made it and I shakily got into the driver's seat, took a deep breath, and carefully drove him the few miles to the doctor.

When the doctor examined Bob, he found no evidence of a stroke and tried to question Bob of his symptoms. Bob's mouth still didn't work right, and I had to interpret his answers. The doctor sent us on home, instructing me to make an appointment with our family doctor.

I did as he said, and the doctor was able to see him later that day. By that time the stroke symptoms had vanished, and the doctor simply attributed the spell to a weird effect of the flu.

Instead of improving over the next few days, Bob began to have excruciating headaches, as well as recurring bouts of paralysis. I made another appointment with the doctor.

This visit made an ugly stain on the picture. The doctor called me aside and told me, "Bob isn't really having those headaches—he's just putting on the pain."

I was so shocked at his statement I could have slapped him. I knew my husband better than that! There would be no reason for him to put on pain!

"Just in case," the doctor added ("to make you feel better," he meant), "I'll give you a referral to a neurosurgeon for his opinion."

I made the appointment with the specialist and later that

week drove Bob the thirty minutes to meet with him.

"I'd like to have Bob enter the hospital for tests," he said. "However, no beds are available in my ward for now, but we'll give you a call when one comes up."

We agreed to his plan. But before a bed was ready for Bob, his condition had deteriorated so much that he was out of his head and didn't know what was going on around him, constantly crying out from pain. Stretched beyond my limit, I called the neurosurgeon. "I'm at my wits' end," I told him. "Please do something!"

"Bring Bob on into the hospital, and I'll see that he is admitted," the neurologist said, compassion in his voice. I had to call for help to do this. My two neighbors were home and made a chair out of their hands to carry Bob to the car, where I put him into the backseat. Bob's sister got in back with him and had to literally hold him down as I drove the half hour to the hospital. It was a nightmare I don't ever want to repeat.

When we reached the hospital, they whisked Bob up to a room in the specialist's ward, and I sank to the floor at the doorway while they got him into bed and gave him an injection to quiet him. I don't even remember driving home, but I got there, relieved that Bob, at least for a while, was resting. Someone could help him now. After missing four nights of sleep because of concern for my husband, I finally slept and ate my first solid meal.

But it got worse. Though the doctor could ease his pain, Bob's hallucinations embraced the weird and sometimes scary. He "saw" a Russian rocketship land outside his window. He made a nurse jump when he yelled, "Watch out, the floor's radioactive!" One day he told me, "You know, I'm never bored. The news comes on that wall across from me on a moving banner" (a la Times Square).

Meanwhile, the neurosurgeon continued to order tests for Bob, to determine what the nature of his illness was so it could be treated.

Then, the worst day of all, the doctor took me into his office to talk to me. "I knew it was some form of meningitis when I first saw Bob," he said. "Hopefully, it would have been the kind caused by a bacteria. Then we could have treated it. Sadly, though, it is a viral meningitis, and we have no treatment for that. Bob could be permanently paralyzed at any time, or he could possibly die. And there's not a thing we can do about it."

I stared at him, disbelieving. This couldn't be true! Doctors could take care of anything that went wrong in our bodies or minds. Couldn't they?

"Not a thing we can do." There was no help for Bob, after all.

But there was, as I was soon to find out.

My sister-in-law suggested I call the pastor of our church. He had married Bob and me nine years previously. We rarely attended services, being "too busy" with other things, such as a beach trip or a football game on TV. Or sleeping in. Or . . . most anything. I should have been embarrassed to call him, but I was too frantic for that, trying to find a way out of this hopeless black tunnel.

The pastor came to the hospital that very same day. It was not one of Bob's better days, whatever "better" meant at that point, but he seemed to recognize the pastor at first sight. Bob looked at the man and said, "They won't tell me the truth, but I know you will. Am I already dead, or am I crazy?"

Now, most people would have been shocked at that question, and unable to answer, or at least stumbling in response. Not this pastor. Without hesitation he answered, "God tells us in His Word that He has not given us the spirit of fear, but of power, and of love, and of a sound mind."

Bob's response to this: "Oh."

The pastor continued to give God's Word to Bob that day, and the next, and every day after. No, there was not instant healing for Bob, but the hallucinations dwindled and stopped, and his weak arm and hand grew stronger. Soon Bob was helped to sit in a chair, and eventually he began to walk short distances, then longer and longer.

For four weeks the doctor continued with painful spinal taps, measuring his blood pressure, taking his temperature to check for infection. At last he was declared ready to return home. That was a happy day for all the family and me (an understatement). There were frequent trips back to the hospital for more spinal taps after that, and plenty of bed rest, but gradually Bob's strength returned until, four months from the time he first took ill, the neurosurgeon called him in for a final checkup and dismissal. As Bob walked in to the doctor's office, the surgeon stood up and walked around his desk to grasp Bob's hand. "My star patient!" he declared. The doctor had his own happy day. He gave Bob permission to return to work, half days at first, and said he didn't have to come back to the hospital for any more checkups.

Through the faithful preaching of God's Word, both Bob and I were able to see how God Himself was our Shelter in the time of storm, and as Psalm 46:1 tells us, "our very present help in trouble."

No, Bob wasn't paralyzed, nor did he die. He began to study for the ministry, and he eventually became a pastor, giving back to others in their time of trouble. His testimony of his own deliverance by our faithful God has always been an inspiration to others, leading many to see that God was their own Shelter in their time of storm, sometimes the only Shelter, but always the best.

20

ONE GOOD HOMBRE

MELANIE H. PLATT

His name is Hombre, and he comes with big teeth, fast kicks, and a bad attitude. Little did I know that God would use this recalcitrant creature to answer a whole litany of prayers that I had poured out in pleading, in anger, and in total defeat over the past several years. The headaches that gripped me periodically were about to turn loose of my life.

Hombre's jumping skills made him a good horse to learn on, and while he terrified us students, our instructor could manage him with no qualms. As she saddled him up and slid the bit in his mouth, I studied him and pondered my dream from the night before. It had been a strange contradiction of emotions and scenes. I remembered feeling completely peaceful as I tumbled from Hombre's back, falling gently through the air and waking up just before I hit the ground. We often change the horses we ride in class, and in several months of lessons I had never been on Hombre before. Why would a horse I had never ridden invade my dreams one night, and how unlikely was it that I would be assigned to him the next day?

In spite of assurances that Hombre's bad behavior didn't continue once he walked into the arena, I did my best not to fidget with my reins and irritate him. He seemed responsive and willing enough, and by the end of class I was enjoying our lesson. Our last goal of the day was to canter over a six-inch cross rail, and I felt good as we landed lightly and balanced. Yet after just a stride, something went wrong. I found myself thrown onto Hombre's neck, staring down at the far-away dirt, and having the sudden thought that I could fall off. That thought abruptly came true when Hombre bucked again.

My next sight came over the toes of my boots as I lay in the gritty sand. I could see a fellow student standing next to her horse and looking down at me, her expression sober. My instructor knelt beside me, asking if I was all right. Because I had landed on my back and knocked the wind out of myself, I couldn't reply. I nodded slightly, struggling for that moment when the air would rush back into my body.

"Can you move your legs?" came the worried question. Still I couldn't answer, so I waved my leg and my arm in the air, and that movement brought blessed oxygen into my flattened lungs.

"Okay," I managed to gasp.

I could tell the exact spot on my pelvis that suffered the brunt of the fall, and while I could move without much discomfort, I knew from experience that worse things were to come. My head had not been involved in the crash, but I got up slowly, unsure whether I was going to be dizzy. All of my body parts were still working, although they felt a bit shakier than before. I got back on Hombre, according to the rule about the best thing to do when you fall off a horse, and cantered one more lap before I quit for the day.

By chance, my regular monthly chiropractic appointment was on Monday. I managed to ice, heat, and ibuprofen my way through the weekend until I could get checked out. I'd been visiting Dr. Roberts for several months, hoping to find relief for the migraines that periodically greeted me when I woke up. While the headaches were manageable with medication, I wanted to be pill and pain free. The regular adjustments hadn't fixed my problem, but they reduced the intensity of the events. At this appointment I wasn't concerned about my headaches but my vertebrae. A collection of black and heavy bruises inked my lower back. Amazingly, nothing had been seriously damaged in my fall, no fractures or disc damage to be found. However my sacroiliac joint, where the spine and the pelvis join, had suffered a sprain.

Dr. Roberts did some manipulation, gave me a series of exercises to do, and warned me about relapses. Three days later it did relapse with a vengeance. I woke up with an ache that contracted into sharp spasms when I tried to slink out of bed. I hobbled in to the chiropractic office like an old lady with rocks in her orthopedics. The initial thrill of avoiding serious injuries felt considerably less comforting that day. What if things were going to get still worse? My imagination came up with scenarios of constant pain and disability. Until I remembered my strange dream, and the peace I felt while falling. No coincidence could explain my dreaming about Hombre right before I rode him, and surely that surreal feeling of contentment while falling meant something, too.

The doctor did several more adjustments that day, and

then my back began to heal in earnest. Just two weeks later I gave up my heating pad and found I could ride with no discomfort.

"How's the back?" Dr. Roberts asked a month later, as I sat once again on the table.

"It seems fine. And I only had the slightest headache for one day." It had been a good month all up and down my spine. The next month I didn't have any headaches at all. It was the next pain-free month when I realized I wasn't just having a grace period; I was healed. Except for times when I'm fighting a lot of stress and get too tense, or if I neglect to do my stretches, my headaches have been gone. Somehow falling on my lower back changed things in my neck and head.

The diagnosis of no fractures or serious injuries makes my soul grateful. I am thrilled and rejoice at being freed from biting headaches. But it's the feeling of peace that God shared with me in my dream that fills me with a rich sense of being blessed.

I don't mind Hombre's bad attitude when I go out to the barn. If God thinks he's worthy to be used for doing good, so do I. God took a bad moment on an ornery horse to give me an extra dollop of His love. How like Him to answer my prayers in a way no human would ever consider. How unexpected of Him to give me supernatural comfort and encouragement in a dream. God used my crash in the dirt to strengthen my trust and bless me, and that leaves me laughing and awestruck at the same time.

21

WHEN SHEEP FLY

DIANE NUNLEY

"Thanks, Penny; another great class. See you in two years!" I hated to give up a Saturday for required CPR training, but this year it was my only option. I was a nurse on leave from my position at my husband's clinic. I wanted to be available to help my ailing parents. On Monday, I had workers arriving to begin a major remodeling project at my home. On Wednesday, I spent some time in my yard pruning shrubs to allow the workers easier access to the house. My enemy, the wasp, stung my hand with a vengeance. My activities and the efforts of the carpenters preparing for the new addition had disturbed their nests. I was scheduled to attend a daylong conference on Thursday, and my eighty-four-year-old dad offered to house-sit, take care of the dog, and work in the vegetable garden while I attended the seminar. I had an outpatient surgery on my foot scheduled on Friday. I prayed for strength of spirit and body to help me through another busy week.

The morning of the seminar, I awoke with the room spinning. I assessed myself and determined I might be having a reaction to the bee sting I had encountered the day before. Having just reviewed the symptoms of a heart attack the week prior, I was confident that a cardiac event was not my problem. Now my hand started to swell. Between the nausea and the pains in my hand and foot, I felt stressed. The house was literally torn up, my driveway was gone, and I had to get out early in the morning. I prayed, "Dear Lord! Get me through this!" I remembered, *The Lord is my shepherd.* I knew He would guide me.

I started to feel better but not well enough to attend my seminar. I planned to call Dad to tell him I would be home all day, and if he still wanted to work the garden, he could arrive at his leisure instead of the agreed time of 8 a.m. I thanked the Lord for getting me through my little episode and pondered His recent encouragement to meditate on the 23rd Psalm. As a Sunday school teacher for more than thirty years, I was embarrassed. He didn't ask me to memorize Zephaniah or have some deep mystery revealed to me from Revelation. Psalm 23? Shouldn't I be "beyond" David's most famous poem? For nearly three months, I had meditated on this during my morning quiet time. I repeated it as I dressed in the morning, reviewed it at lunch, and recited it again before retiring. The Lord impressed new meanings and greater depths regarding His relationship with His sheep. Like David when he prayed this prayer, I was now older with a rich history of God's provisions and care for me. I wondered, *What is He preparing me for?*

My mom called and told me to expect my dad at any minute. He was nearly two hours early. He arrived in only a few minutes and stood at the door holding a heating pad. "Come on in, Pops. I'm sorry I didn't catch you before you left. I won't be going today, and you could have stayed home." He headed for my sofa. "What's with the heating pad?" This was August! He looked serious when he said, "I feel like I may be getting pleurisy again. I thought I would sit here and use some heat for a while." The bells went off inside my nurse's head. Pops had nearly died from pneumonia the previous year. This complaint could be serious. He had no other symptoms. His breathing seemed normal. My doctor husband talked briefly with him and suggested I take him to our local rural hospital for a chest film.

I quickly dressed, and my concern for my dad jolted me into feeling well. Not in any big rush, Dad stopped to admire the roses and chat with the workmen. Then we drove to the hospital, a ten-minute ride away. I let him out at the ER entrance where he would sign in for an outpatient X-ray. Parking the car and walking into the building took less than five minutes.

I arrived to see Pops signing the mounds of paperwork required for his X-ray. He made a joke about being thankful he could still get medical care at his age. Then he put down the pen and slumped over in the chair. I was stunned! Checking his carotid pulse and finding none, I assessed he was not breathing. "Call a code!" I hollered. The clerk was also shocked. He had been in her chair for just a few minutes.

Penny, my CPR instructor, arrived with a wheelchair and together we lifted Pops into the seat. The relief I felt to see her was immeasurable. Fortunately for my dad, the emergency room was only around the corner and CPR was in progress within seconds. Intravenous lines, oxygen, and monitors were placed, and he was defibrillated immediately when ventricular fibrillation was observed. My dad and I had discussed end-of-life issues. I had power of attorney over both of my parents' health issues. He said he did not want to end up on "machines," and I respected that. Yet, with the immediate proximity of technology, I didn't hesitate to intervene. CPR continued for twenty minutes.

As I waited, I was accompanied by two former colleagues who were also Christians. I asked one of them to go to my dad, whisper in his ear during the resuscitation efforts, and present the gospel one more time. Knowing the sense of hearing is the last to fail, I believed it couldn't hurt to try one last time. A few minutes later, she came back into the room and said, "I told him. He's now in normal sinus rhythm! He's intubated and sedated, and we're shipping him to his cardiologist in Nashville!" I was even more stunned. After forty years as a nurse, I knew the odds of surviving CPR at his age were poor.

The helicopter pilot was a familiar face from our local airport where my husband and I keep our small private plane. He agreed to let me fly with my dad. My little band of supporters gathered for prayer, and we loaded Dad into the helicopter. The two flight nurses who received my dad were obviously proficient and well trained. I was beginning to see the events of the morning through David's pen: *I shall not want for anything.* My dad had been moved along by the unseen Hand in a way I could not have designed myself.

I began to reflect. *The Lord is my shepherd.* No kidding! He led us "right on the money" today. If we had encountered a red light, Pops would have arrested in my car and likely would have been dead by the time we arrived at the hospital. *I shall not want.* The entire event at the hospital could have easily been one of those training films where everything works out perfectly and leaves the seasoned viewers cynically laughing. Yet everything my dad needed was within seconds of reach, and all the appropriate personnel were standing by.

The two flight nurses remarked how calm I appeared sitting in "the bird." I corrected the pilot on the destination hospital and asked for an ETA, estimated time of arrival. They questioned my familiarity with the environment, and I confessed to my two "angels" that I was an old nurse and also a private pilot. If I didn't think about my dad being the patient, this could have been just another "day in paradise," a term used to describe a day that stressed a nurse to the limits. The sweet calm the Spirit gives had enveloped me, and even though I was in a familiar element, I credited my peace to the One who gives peace that surpasses all understanding. My dad was deeply sedated on life support, but all his vital signs were normal.

He maketh me to lie down in green pastures. We lifted off over the green pastures of our middle Tennessee home, and I thanked the Lord for all the good progress as I monitored my dad lying flat on the stretcher. *He leadeth me beside the still waters.* Looking out the window, I saw the glisten of the early morning fog lifting off the Duck River. *He restores my soul.* Right then, his condition appeared favorable. *He leads me in paths of righteousness for His name's sake.* Boy, did I have a story to tell! *Yea, though I walk through the valley of the shadow of death, I will fear no evil.* We had been there. *Thy rod and thy staff, they comfort me.* The receiving Level One hospital complimented our rural team for a job well done.

You prepare a table before me in the presence of mine enemies. You anoint my head with oil. I praised God for the anointing oil of modern technology that intervened in the life of an eighty-four-year-old man. We were later told by his cardiologist that there is little data on eighty-four-year-olds who successfully survive full arrest. *My cup runneth over.* I was full with gratitude that the Lord had kept me home that day. Canceling my plans allowed me to be available to get my dad to the hospital at exactly the right time. *Surely goodness and mercy shall follow me all the days of my life. And I shall dwell in the house of the Lord forever.* We landed, were escorted to the CCU, and found his cardiologist standing at the nurses' desk waiting for us. He just "happened" to be on call. The night nurse, Kelly, knew my dad because she accompanied his doctor to our rural hospital where patients are seen each month. What a blessing to see a familiar face so far from home!

My dad had one stint placed, was off life support by the afternoon, had a defibrillator implanted the next morning, and was home that weekend. Even though my hand was twice the normal size, my foot surgery had to be postponed, and my house was a disaster, I was overjoyed to have my dad still with us. He completed his cardiac rehabilitation during the next few months. As of this writing, he is eighty-eight and still gardening. I continue to learn from the Lord about how He prepares us, calling us to obedience. His call to me to study Psalm 23, which was vividly revealed in the events I experienced, affirmed His personal watchful care, grace, and love. The Spirit envelops us and comforts us with words that cannot be uttered. Obedience to the Lord in small things may culminate in a collision of a big event, like a puzzle; it all comes together in His appointed time. I am thankful for my training, which prompted me to have my patient positioned for early intervention with a life-threatening arrhythmia. Yet, I am ultimately thankful to have been held like one of David's sheep and guided by His hand. Since then, when I face a troublesome situation, I remind myself of how the Lord arrives exactly on time. The Lord showed me that day I can truly be "anxious for nothing." He will provide. By making our requests known to God, the peace that surpasses all understanding is available to all of His sheep.

22

IRIS BLESSING

BONNIE MAE EVANS

Sorrow swept over me in a familiar wave that threatened to drown me as I sat kneeling in the dirt. Staring into the hole we had just dug for the iris bulbs, I thought, *That's how I feel, empty, like there's a hole where my heart should be.*

Today was a joyous day for our friends, Cindy and Tom, for whom I was babysitting. Moments earlier they had backed out of our driveway excitedly waving good-bye to two-year-old Paige, who stood beside me. I waved back, trying hard to share their joy while carefully hiding my pain.

They were on their way to the hospital for the scheduled delivery of their second child, another daughter, already named Sophie Louise. It seemed to me that they were able to plan out every detail of their lives like clockwork.

Exactly five years after their marriage, their goal of buying a house and saving a nest egg of a predetermined amount reached, they had their first daughter, Paige. Now, two years later, once again following their carefully laid-out plan, they were on the way to the hospital to have their second daughter at a scheduled time. They knew ahead of time. They could make a plan and follow it.

Unlike my life. My life felt uncontrollable, riddled with ups and downs resembling a runaway roller coaster. The only thing I was able to plan were visits to the infertility specialist, followed by the necessary surgeries and tests.

My heart ached as little hands gently took the iris bulb from mine and daintily pushed it into the waiting hole. A tear slid down my cheek and dripped into the dirt after it, watering the bulb with my pain. We planted several more in a row when Paige quietly broke through my thoughts. She took my hand.

"Let's say a prayer for them to grow, Missa Bonna."

I had my doubts that they would grow at all in the sandy soil of this semi-tropical climate. They, like me, were transplants here in South Carolina. My mother had dug them out of the rich black soil around her home in the north and sent them with me when we moved, a little piece of home.

I looked into the sweet, innocent face looking up at me expectantly and smiled.

"What a nice idea, Paige. Let's do that," I said, patting her tiny hands in mine. Oh, how I longed for a little one of my own to plant flower bulbs and say prayers over them with.

Closing our eyes, as Paige prayed out loud, I prayed silently.

Dear God, please give me a sign if I will ever have a baby. If I know, then I can get on with my life, but just not knowing, always hoping, has become unbearable. If I am to have a child someday, please make these irises bloom this year. Amen.

Being a new Christian in the Bible belt, I had recently heard of "casting out the fleece" when looking for an answer and decided to give it a try. I believed with every fiber of my being that God "is able to do far more abundantly beyond all that we ask or think, according to the power that works within us," as I remembered reading in Ephesians 3:20 (NASB). But, I also knew that His will is not always ours and that His ways are not our ways. God has a plan for our lives, and it is important to let God be God. After all, He knows everything about our past, present, and future.

Months passed, and I forgot about that prayer, but God remembered. Bright and early on Easter morning the following spring, my husband, Bill, and I hurried out to the car to leave for church. As I turned to get into the car, my heart leaped at what was in front of me. There in the forgotten flower bed stood two gorgeous purple irises fully bloomed. Excitedly, I told my husband about my prayer and how the irises were God's answer. He smiled what appeared to be a patronizing smile, but I was sure this was a promise. I could tell he wasn't all that sure.

Another year and a half rolled by with no baby. But I was okay with the waiting now because in my heart I knew that eventually I would have a baby. I just had to wait for God's perfect timing. My husband's time in the navy was over, so we moved back north to Maryland, reluctantly leaving friends behind that had become like family to us.

We both got busy securing jobs. Finally, after being married seven years, we were able to purchase our first home. Each night as I went upstairs to bed, I stood and gazed longingly into the spare room, desperately hoping it would be a nursery someday soon.

My doctor in Charleston referred me to an infertility specialist at Johns Hopkins Hospital in Baltimore, where I continued to have treatments, procedures, and the latest and greatest medicines on the market. Months dissolved into years. One year disappeared into the next. Somewhere along the way, about seven years after we first started our infertility workup, I lost hope and fell into despair. My dream of having a family of my own was slipping away. I no longer remembered God's promise.

One day while I was dragging myself around a craft fair with a friend, my eyes fell on a lovely watercolor painting. It portrayed a delicate violet sharing a stem with a bud that had not yet bloomed. Psalm 37:4 was written all along the stem and leaves: "Delight yourself in the LORD; and He will give you the desires of your heart" (NASB).

That's it! I thought. *All I need to do is delight myself in the Lord more, and then I will surely have a baby!* Quickly paying for the picture, I took it home and hung it on our bedroom wall so that it was the first thing my eyes focused on in the morning. Praying and reading my Bible, I worked joyfully at church and witnessed to others, delighting myself in the Lord.

Two more years passed, and a strange thing began to happen. I realized my "delight" was taking on a life of its own. My heart's desire had become whatever God's plan was for my life. My own agenda was no longer of importance.

Around this time, our church was planning a medical mission trip to Rwanda, Africa. My husband and I, being a dentist and a nurse, decided after praying about it that this must be what God had planned for us, so we signed up to go. We attended the planning and informational meetings. There would be a lot to do and only a short time to get it all accomplished. Many immunizations were needed. In order to get them all before we left they had to be scheduled right away. I scheduled our appointments. I had been feeling a bit under the weather lately. Just to be sure before getting the immunizations, my doctor drew blood for a pregnancy test. Surprise of all surprises! It came back positive!

Finally, after fifteen years of marriage, nine years of infertility treatments, thirty thousand dollars, five surgeries, two failed in vitro fertilization attempts, and tests and procedures too numerous to recall, I was actually pregnant!

We would not be going to Rwanda after all. God had another plan. It had been nine long years since I prayed that prayer, prompted by a precious little girl.

My doctor handled my case very cautiously and tried to keep my excitement at bay by warning me that "older" mothers had a higher risk of miscarriage. He had seen my disappointment too many times before. Much to his surprise, except for a bad case of morning sickness, I breezed through those nine months.

We left for the hospital on a Saturday night under a beautiful full moon. Our daughter, Hillary, was born the next evening on Easter Sunday, after twenty-six hours of labor. God had not only kept His promise, but He even told me what *day* she would be born on! But there was still more to come.

Five years later, only a month after my husband and I

celebrated our twentieth anniversary, our son, Will, was born. Once again, I remembered God's promise to me through the irises. I marveled at how specific He had been in His answer. Two irises bloomed that Easter morning, representing each of my children.

During my darkest times of despair, I forgot the promise He gave me, but I learned to desire His will for my life. In relinquishing my will to His, He gave me the desires of my heart.

My daughter is now twenty-four years old, and my son is eighteen. My hubby and I are still in awe of our extraordinary God who extends His grace to us each day and is able to do exceedingly, abundantly above all that we could ever ask or hope for! To Him we give all the glory. He alone is worthy of all our praise!

23

PROMISES TO KEEP

SCOTT STANLEY,
AS TOLD TO SHARON SHEPPARD

The hot Nebraska air hung heavy with humidity. My family and I were riding along a country road outside of Lincoln when the cell phone rang.

"Scott," the voice said, "Joan, from the Mayo Clinic. We have a heart."

Above the hum of the engine, I hesitated, not sure I had heard right. A heart transplant offered virtually my only hope of surviving long enough to see my kids grow up. As a thirty-seven-year-old dad, I had determined to grab that chance if and when it came.

Ever since the doctors had told me three months earlier that they had done everything they could for me, I longed for some glimmer of hope. Yet, when it came, it caught me off guard. A few days earlier, the heart transplant coordinator at had estimated this opportunity wouldn't come up for another three to six months. I hoped I could hang on that long.

"We need you here in three hours, Scott. Four at the most," she said.

"We've got a heart," I relayed the message to my wife, Cheri.

"Primary or secondary?" she asked.

"Primary."

The clinic generally lines up two recipients for a given heart, assigning priority on the basis of urgency and which person is the better match. Summoning both patients to the Mayo, the medical team preps the secondary patient in case the primary recipient doesn't make it or for some reason isn't deemed healthy enough at the last minute to survive the procedure. On this particular night, June 13, 2005, my name rose to the top of the list.

After months of prior testing, five stop-gap surgeries over a period of time, and numerous car trips to Rochester, Minnesota, we now had to figure out how to make the 350-mile trip from Nebraska in three hours' time. Unfortunately, on this particular evening, the clinic's MayoAir jet was grounded by a severe local thunderstorm.

"We'll figure something out," I assured the coordinator.

During the next couple of chaotic hours, Cheri tossed a few clothes into a bag and arranged for her mother to keep our sons, three-year-old Blake and five-year-old Chase.

My wife and my father and I, all on separate cell phones, frantically dialed from our list of private plane owners, hitting one dead end after another in our attempts to find transportation. Eventually we connected with a pilot and an UltraAir corporate turbojet out of Moline, Illinois.

Frequent trips to the Mayo had kept me away from our preschoolers far more than any of us would have liked, but following my return home a few days earlier, I had promised Blake and Chase that now I'd be home for the next thirty days.

A breathing crisis over the weekend had landed me in our local hospital, so by the time I left for Minnesota around 11:30 the night of the phone call, I had spent less than twenty-four hours at home with the boys.

With little time for lingering farewells, I fervently hugged our two sons, neither of whom had any idea that this could be the last time they'd see their father alive. As the small plane taxied down the airstrip, Chase stood on the runway crying. "But, Daddy," he yelled, "you said you'd be home for thirty days! You *promised!*"

My faulty heart thudded during the hour-and-a-half flight, and as I contemplated the ramifications of a transplant, the thought that someone had to die so I could live haunted me.

I was nearly thirty before I had any inkling something might be wrong with my heart. I'd been vigorous, athletic, and ambitious. As superintendent of a golf course, I worked eighteen-hour days and gave little thought to my health. I loved my work.

My grandfather had owned a golf course, and, in that community if your last name was Stanley, you played golf. People sometimes chuckle when I say that I majored in golf at college, but I actually earned an A.S. degree in golf course turf management. Superintending golf courses became my career.

Until my diagnosis, I had never heard of hypertrophic cardiomyopathy (HCM), a congenital heart disease that affects about one in five hundred people. As the muscular walls of the ventricles become abnormally thickened, the disease can cause a variety of heart problems, not the least of which is sudden death. For the past seven years, I had lived with that possibility.

After we touched down in Rochester, an ambulance whisked me from the airport to St. Mary's Hospital, where the medical team waited. Fluid on my lungs added pulmonary complications to the procedure. Just before they wheeled me into surgery, one of the transplant cardiologists said, "Scott, there are no guarantees with this. You need to know that you may not make it off the table."

"I will," I said. "I've got to."

I'm a stubborn guy, and for once in my life, I discovered that can be an asset. There's nothing in the world like a couple of kids to motivate a dad to live. I knew I couldn't leave Cheri to raise them alone.

Before becoming a father, I never dreamed I could love kids the way I love Chase and Blake. These boys and their mother had become everything to me. That night I knew it could all quickly come to an end.

I went into surgery at 3:30 a.m. An expert team of specialists removed my faulty heart and replaced it with one that had so recently been removed from the chest of its young donor. Three hours after the procedure began, my new heart was up and running. By 11:30 that morning, the team moved me into ICU.

When the haze of anesthesia eventually cleared, I felt nauseated. Vomiting with a tube down the throat is miserable at best. But my first waking thought was, *I made it! I'm alive.*

My wife is my best friend, and through it all, she's been a rock. Cheri slept at the hospital for two weeks. Because I couldn't talk with the ventilator tube in my throat, the nurse brought me an alphabet card so I could communicate by spelling out words.

After my release, I spent the next couple of months at Gift of Life Transplant House in Rochester, a home-like facility that provides housing for transplant patients and their caregivers. The hours grew long. Possibly the most difficult part of the whole ordeal was the tedium of those weeks of recovery. I'd always been a go-er. All my life I'd been driven. Now during the slow days of recuperation I felt depressed and useless.

"Why me?" I asked.

I suppose a guy can't go through these kinds of crises without some heavy-duty soul searching. As the days stretched into weeks, I had plenty of time to think. Probably the biggest attitude shift came in the way I learned to value more highly my faith and my family.

While working on the golf course, my church attendance had slipped. Weekends were busy on the course, and I joked that I worshiped at the Chapel of the Eighteen Holes every Sunday. But coming face-to-face with death helped me to gain a new perspective on the fact that God must have a plan for my life. I know I'd never have made it through all of this without His help.

Our lives are quite different now. Our roles have reversed. Cheri has taken an outside job, and I'm holding the fort at home. I've gained a whole new appreciation for stay-at-home moms. I had no idea what a difficult job it can be.

I may never know the age or gender or identity of my donor, or the circumstances of the donor's death, but I will be forever grateful for a second chance at life. For months I agonized about how to say thanks to my unknown donor's family. Words are so woefully inadequate. Finally, I wrote a letter that the transplant coordinator agreed to forward to them, telling a little about my family and what it has meant to me to have the incredible chance to raise my boys. I told them I am deeply humbled, and I promised the family I would not abuse this gift. At the end I simply said, "Thank you for the gift of life."

While recuperating in Rochester, I told the transplant coordinator my goal was to make it home in time to see our son off to his first day of kindergarten. This pushed the limits a bit, she thought, but I pleaded. Couldn't I at least have a pass to go home for a few days? I had promised my son I'd be there, and that was a promise I didn't intend to break.

I got home on Friday. On Monday, August 29, on an extraordinarily beautiful, sunny day, I walked the four blocks with Chase to school. I watched as kids from up and down the street streamed into the schoolyard, dressed in their new first-day-of-school clothes. Chase eased into the crowd and, with a wave, disappeared behind the heavy doors. I wouldn't have missed this for the world.

"My daddy walked to school with me today," he told his class that first day. "He's got a new heart."

Indeed, I have. In more ways than one.

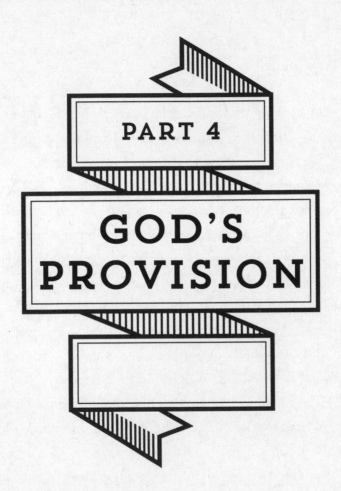

PART 4

GOD'S PROVISION

24

LAUGHING LORD OF LOVE

SHELDON K. BASS

It was a gloriously special time in life, when God was revealing Himself to His newly reborn child of thirty earth years. We were getting well acquainted. I had questions, yet I was determined to remain true to my commitment to Christ, no matter what the answers to my questions would be. The setting was a picturesque, mountainous region of North Carolina, where I'd been led by the Spirit to relocate. Spiritually, I was up on the mountain of God, in His presence, where there's great joy and all needs are miraculously provided for.

If I was to then live a life that pleases my Lord, every action taken was vitally important, every word spoken scrutinized, and every thought weighed in the balance.

"Heavenly Father, what parts of my character are okay to keep? What about my sense of humor? You know how I love to make people laugh."

How does God feel about such things? Does Jesus laugh? I asked Him.

"Lord, do you have a sense of humor?"

Unknowingly, I had just enlisted for a three-day affair of side-splitting hilarity. Good thing no other people were around because they might have called for those guys in white coats to come haul me off to the loony bin. I'd never laughed so heartily or for such a lengthy duration.

Seeking the Lord's thoughts on numerous issues, the Bible would enlighten me on most subjects. However, God always offered multiple confirmations, through various modes of delivery, ensuring there would be no misinterpretation. For instance, I'd turn on the radio in my vehicle and a minister would be talking about the exact query I'd just made. Or I'd make a phone call to some person, and they'd unwittingly be right on point, confirming what God had just revealed to me. He also used circumstances as confirmation. There's no sensation in the world so spectacular as the certainty that the one true Deity is communicating, dealing directly with *you*!

As the Spirit compelled me to delve into God's Word, every page I flipped open had me laughing. Humor was our topic of discussion that day. And reading it in that light, searching for whether or not God likes to laugh, I found His multifarious funny bone. Of course, the comedy that makes one person roar might bore another. A superb fact is, that He knows more about us than we do ourselves. He knows precisely what makes *me* chuckle.

"He that sitteth in the heavens shall laugh . . ."
— PSALM 2:4 KJV

It began subtly with poetic justice and irony. Haman had a gallows built, hatching a plot to hang Mordecai, but God took the nefarious scheme and turned the tables on the Jew-hating perpetrator. Haman ended up being hung on the same gallows he'd built for the one he despised (Esther 5:9–7:10).

Those who set a snare for another will be caught in it themselves. Those who roll a stone onto another, it will roll back onto them. It reminded me of the Wile E. Coyote and the Roadrunner cartoons. Every time that determined coyote set a trap for the beep-beeping roadrunner, it would backfire on him. He'd get squashed, fall off a cliff, or get blown up, while his nemesis would escape unscathed. All of a sudden, stuff I'd previously read in the Bible was becoming a whimsical comedy.

"If a man digs a pit, he will fall into it;
if a man rolls a stone, it will roll back on him."
— PROVERBS 26:27 NIV

"The heathen are sunk down in the pit that they made:
in the net which they hid is their own foot taken."
— PSALM 9:15 KJV

A truckload of scriptures proves beyond any skepticism that God indeed has a wonderful sense of humor. Once a person gets to laughing, the funniness has a way of increasing as you go, like a crescendo in music. The climaxing Bible story that nearly knocked me off my chair in gleeful hysteria was where God made Balaam's donkey talk (see Numbers 22).

Yes, I'd found my new best Friend, One I could be myself with, because He already knew all about me. We laughed together, enjoying each other. And we cried and mourned together.

It didn't take much to fill my life. A pickup truck, a few hand tools, and some work clothes made up the bulk of my meager possessions. I was starting over from scratch, and in more ways than one: spiritually, physically, and financially. I had no job and very little money. And it was my first time in North Carolina. Yet there was great contentment and peace, complete satisfaction. And I was experiencing many downright awesome things for the first time. Hey, what could be better than hanging out with the Creator of the cosmos?

My lessons turned to the necessity of frequently gathering together with the body of Christ, my brothers and sisters in the Lord. Until then it'd been just Jesus and me; I hadn't been to church for a while.

After driving around Rutherford County, searching for just the right church, the Spirit pointed out the one to visit that coming Sunday. I was eager and excited—until Sunday rolled around.

My suitcase of dress clothes had gotten wet; everything was covered with mildew. I had to throw out the only decent set of clothes I'd brought along. Neither did I have the money to purchase a new outfit. So I polished some cowboy boots, brushed off my best jeans, and put on a clean shirt. Driving into the church lot, I noticed all the expensive shiny new cars. Then I saw the people headed inside all duded up in their fancy, Sunday-go-to-meetin' clothes.

It was a lousy time to notice that the bed of my rusted-out

Chevy was all trashed up. Then, comparing my clothes to the garb of my siblings in Christ, I turned around in shame and headed straight back out of the parking lot. I turned toward my rented cracker box, with grapefruit-sized holes in the floor, which I had dubbed the "holy trailer."

I was embarrassed to go into church but also ashamed before my best Friend because I'd acted like a coward. So, having just recently learned of His sense of humor, I decided to use that to my advantage.

"Father, I'm sorry. I was ashamed to go in there looking like this. My hair needs cut—I look like a hippie. But Lord, I'm Your child. If You really want Your kid to go in there looking like he just fell off the hobo train . . . well . . . then, I promise I'll go to church next week. But if it's all right with You, I could sure use some new church clothes."

I had just given my *amen* to that short prayer, when I drove past the community dumpsters. Turning around, I drove back to clean out the back of my truck.

There, hanging on the outside of one garbage bin, were three men's suits, like new, still in their plastic wrap from the dry cleaners. Someone who'd had a yard sale had left them where people could see them. No need to even ask; they all three fit as if they'd been custom-tailored to my body. Tears mingled with joyous laughter over God's answer to my prayer, blurring my vision as I headed home. I kept having to pull off the road to clear my eyes. It was as if He was saying, "How do you like them apples?" The haircut, too, was provided by God, through my sister, who lived fifteen miles to the north.

Every day was now filled with miracles, each flowing on the heels of the previous. And finally God said it was time to find another job; vacation time was over. But I wasn't prepared for how quickly cold weather set in. Unbeknownst to me, the radiator in my truck had lost its antifreeze. With the first overnight freeze, the motor block on my truck froze and cracked. It could only be driven short distances; I had to stop intermittently to add water. I had failed to be a good steward of God's pickup truck. How was I going to get back and forth to work, once a job was even found? I pleaded for forgiveness and His grace.

Waking up Monday morning, the Spirit instructed me to head into town. Strolling down the Mayberry-looking Main Street of Rutherfordton, elation bubbled up inside me over the down-home charm and warmth of its people. I stood agape, peering into the drugstore, which sported a café with an old-fashioned soda fountain. A young man with a neat appearance approached and introduced himself. It seems people in these small towns all know what's going on with everyone else. He already knew I was the brother of Brenda Ellison and I'd come here from Florida.

The fellow happened to be the town manager of Rutherfordton. He asked, "Are you going to be staying here for a while? Perhaps you might need a job?"

"Yes, sir, I was just considering going back to work."

"Forgive me for being so forward, but we're in need of someone to do the upkeep on our four city parks. You'd be the head of parks and recreation. Only thing is, we have a service truck allotted for this position, and we don't have room for it at the motor pool. You'd have to drive it back and forth from your home every day. I hope that wouldn't be a problem."

The Lord's fingerprints were all over this thing. I'd never said anything to anyone about me looking for work or about my cracked motor block. Instantly, I had a job, transportation, and even a flashy new title. And I never even had to fill out an application or ask a soul. Well, I did ask God. And when He's on your side . . . .

When my first check arrived, I took it into the bank to cash it. The teller said she didn't need to see my identification. "We all know who you are, Sheldon."

Wow, I'm among real country folk, where a man's word and a handshake still mean something! I love it! No wonder You wanted me to come here, Lord. You knew I would enjoy the glorious mountains and streams nearby, and adore this quaint little town, and fit right in with its people!

God has led me many places since I first fell in love with my Creator. But that special time, which I like to call our honeymoon period, has given me absolute assurance that He is always with me, that He cares deeply for me, and that He's all powerful. Which means, I can comfortably trust Him with my life. Besides, He makes me laugh!

25

TRUST ME FOR MORE

DONNA SCALES

My teenage son, Scott, came bounding into the kitchen. "Mom! Mom! I found it. I *finally* found it!" His eyes danced with excitement, and an ear-to-ear grin consumed his face. I paid special attention to his ears. Sure enough, they went up. When Scott's grin was full, his ears went up an inch. Right now they were as high as I'd ever seen them.

"What have you found?"

"A welding class! I found a welding class. God finally found one for me."

For three years Scott and I had asked everywhere we went if anyone knew about a welding class. We'd been asking God, too. But, if He knew, He wasn't telling. Until now.

Scott explained, "I talked to a lady on the bus coming home from my job. Her son took a welding class. Here, she wrote it down for me."

Scott handed me a slip of paper. It had *PCC-Rock Creek* written on it. Scott was in high school and PCC was a college, Portland Community College. Rock Creek Campus was way—and I mean *way*—across town. My first reaction was, *Oh my, Jesus, this isn't going to be easy, is it?*

We exchanged a robust high five, and I responded, "I'm

happy for you, honey. You searched a long time for this class. I'll call and find out more."

Many high school students take community college classes but few students who are in special education like Scott was. He has Williams Syndrome. He can't read, do math, read a bus schedule, or make change. But he is abundantly gifted in enthusiasm, guts, and perseverance.

Before I called PCC-Rock Creek, I prayed, *Okay, Lord, here we go. Please guide our path.* So as not to break Scott's heart, or mine, I told them up front about Scott's disability. The welding department director still agreed to meet with us.

It took an hour to drive to the school and another thirty minutes to find the welding department on the sprawled-out campus. The director welcomed us enthusiastically and personally guided us through the various stations of his program. I was overwhelmed. Scott was transfixed.

"Sir, can I take a welding class?" Scott asked eagerly.

"Well, Scott, I'll get you an entrance packet for you to study. Then you'll need to take an entry exam."

Uh-oh! Red light. Stop.

Fighting the tightness in my throat, I quietly said, "Scott can't read."

The director smiled as he handed me the materials for the entrance exam and replied, "Well, let's give it a try. I'll read the exam to him." Then he went back into his office and came out with another packet. It was a copy of the test. "Here, *this* will help you study."

Walking back to the car, Scott was skipping and shouting

while I fought back tears and couldn't speak, anticipating the disappointment that lay ahead. At home I glanced through the test Scott needed to take. My heart sank further. There were words like *oxyacetylene*, *voltage*, and *amperage*. One question read: "Compare and contrast a transformer power source and a transformer rectified power source." *Are you kidding me? Scott hasn't got a chance.*

Lord, I *can't understand any of this. How can I help Scott study?* God seemed to answer, *Donna, I've brought you this far. Trust Me for more.*

So, not even understanding what I was reading, I studied the materials with Scott. He seemed to have a natural understanding. *I wonder where that came from?*

Scott came out of the examination room jumping up and down, shouting for the world to hear, "I passed! I passed!" Following Scott through the door was the director with a sheepish grin on his face. Then out came another man who walked over, reached out to shake my hand, and said, "Hi, my name is Mike. The director introduced me to Scott, and we sort of clicked. I'm a graduate welding student, and I wondered if I could tutor Scott with his welding?" *Wow, God, You did it again—the impossible.* In my mind, there was no doubt God had hand-picked the director of that welding department just to receive our son.

As Scott and I drove home we inventoried God's blessings: He found a welding program for Scott. He provided a welding program director who was willing to accept a boy with intellectual disabilities. He instilled in Scott just enough welding potential to pass the entry test. And, our cup overflowing, He threw in a tutor who could personally guide Scott to maximum success and safety.

For days we reveled in euphoria. I was spreading out bus schedules and maps to plan a route to Rock Creek Campus, when the phone rang. It was the welding director. "Mrs. Scales, I'm sorry to give you this news, but the director of Students with Disabilities has not approved Scott as a student."

"But, but . . . But he's a student with disabilities!"

"I know, but . . . ." He explained as best he could. It was obvious he was trying to be as diplomatic as possible, yet he couldn't hide his frustration. He told me the Disabilities director wanted to meet with me, and he asked (he asked!) if he could attend the meeting also. We set a time. I started praying. *Lord, You've opened this path for Scott. I don't understand this new roadblock, but I choose to trust You. Please fill me with Your Spirit, wisdom to understand, and control of my mouth.*

Mostly when I asked God to control my mouth it meant to keep it shut. For this meeting it was no different. For twenty minutes I answered the Disabilities director's questions, but I didn't volunteer any extra comments. And, yes, that was hard. I began to recognize a theme to all her questions. They centered upon the welding tutor. Finally, I spoke out, "Scott is a rule follower. We feel your rules will keep him safe. We have hired the welding tutor so that Scott will learn the most and not detract from other instruction." Within one minute she assured us Scott could take the class. Her concern had been liability. Scott was in. *Yeah, God!*

Jubilantly I returned to the table full of bus schedules. Our family's priorities dictated that the only option for Scott taking the class was that he get there and back by bus. We felt that the ability to access public transportation was a critical factor to any chance for his future independence. Getting him to and from our city and Rock Creek Campus meant a total of three hours on the bus in order to take a two-hour class. Scott wasn't daunted in the least.

But *I* was. The classes were on Saturday, and it was a complicated route. It took him through three transit centers: two complete bus routes with a transfer in the middle. For Scott to safely learn this route I estimated it would take two months for me to travel-train him—five hours for eight weeks—forty hours of my precious Saturday time. That's when it happened. Despite all God had done to carry us to that point, I got mad. Whiny, self-centered tears replaced happy ones. *Father God, I've given and given and given. Saturdays are the only day I have any time for myself. And now that's being taken away?*

Again, God seemed to whisper, *Trust Me.*

Finally it came, the long-awaited, hard-fought-for first day of welding. Scott was so excited he wiggled all over. I drove him to our local transit center, and he boarded bus 78.

I followed his bus in the car through multiple stops, parked at the Beaverton Transit Center, and was there to meet him as he got off the bus. We walked to ten different bus stops looking for bus 67, the bus he needed to take him to Rock Creek Campus. It couldn't be found. Frustrated, we walked back to bus 78 and asked the bus driver where we could find bus 67.

He gave us an odd smile, stepped off the bus, and pointed to the numbers on his bus. Bus 78 switched numbers to become bus 67 at the Beaverton Transit Center. Scott could get on the bus in our city and stay on the same bus all the way to Rock Creek Campus! The bus driver told us the transit authority had just made that change, that it was quite an unusual procedure, and they only did it on Saturdays.

Scott happily climbed back on the bus and waved to me as he headed to Rock Creek Campus. I pondered what had just happened as I followed his bus. *Let me see if I've got this right. This unique change of procedure involves the very buses Scott needs and only happens on the very day Scott needs it? And they made the change at the very time Scott found a welding class?* God had given me back my Saturdays in a way only He could have planned. Then *I* grinned from ear to ear. I don't know if my ears went up, but I celebrated. *Lord, thank You for putting up with me. I'm sorry for doubting.*

Parked at Rock Creek Campus, I watched as Scott bounced off the bus. He was followed by the bus driver, a big, gentle giant of a man. The two of them walked toward me. Reaching his hand out in greeting, the bus driver said, "Hi, my name is Larry. I have this run for six weeks, and I'll watch out for Scott." Scott was grinning as he happily munched away on a stick of pepperoni that Larry had given him.

Scott took his welding class for a year. Everywhere he went he told people about it. Many marveled that a boy with disabilities could do such a thing. I'm *still* marveling.

It seems unimaginable and impractical that the sovereign

God of the universe would care about the heart's desire of one boy. A welding class wasn't a big thing compared to the woes of many, but God cares about the big stuff of life *and* the smaller stuff.

I try to remember that every time I walk past our heavy, rusted slab of metal that hangs by our front door—Scott's Christmas gift to us that year. It has six letters cut out of the metal by a welding torch—*SCALES*—our family name.

26

THE FAITHFULNESS BASKET

DAWN WILSON

"Ten dollars a month? How's that supposed to work?" The question to my team leader was fair enough, but I just couldn't imagine how God could stretch my meager "pay" to meet all my needs.

In the 1970s, I jumped at the opportunity to sing and serve with a new national revival ministry and travel throughout the United States. During the summer of 1971, this then-twenty-one-year-old arrived at the Life Action Ministries with big dreams, but it didn't take long to realize I wasn't ready to launch into ministry. I wasn't even on the launching pad yet.

The first week, I fell under deep conviction as the evangelist, Del Fehsenfeld Jr., spoke about "Phony Baloney Christianity." I realized I knew all about what Jesus had done for me, but I didn't know Him! In our first high school assembly program in Tampa, Florida, while singing "Do You Know My Jesus?" I broke down in tears.

Overcome by my great spiritual need, I left the stage and fled to the Prayer Room. It was a moment of brokenness and humility—the stirrings of transformation.

In the days to come, I was in awe of how God worked in people's lives: breaking down pride, calling believers to repentance and obedience, restoring families, and changing entire churches. I couldn't believe God had called me to such a powerful ministry.

But I struggled with that ten dollars each team member was allotted for personal needs.

Eventually, Life Action's finances were transformed through an amazing radio-thon fund-raiser. Team members were also encouraged to raise personal support. But in those foundational weeks of ministry, team finances were stretched to their limit. The leadership wanted to help us more, but they simply couldn't.

Some of the other team members received help from their home or friends. I did not. And I soon found myself lacking many practical things like toothpaste, hair spray, deodorant, feminine supplies, nylons, makeup, breath mints, and even thank-you notes to thank the hosts where I would stay each week.

I didn't want to borrow from other team members. I didn't think that would set a good precedent, and, besides, some of them were struggling, too. Although I scrimped and made careful choices, desperation set in as I felt there was no way I could get through another week without the most basic needs. At that point, I even considered leaving the team. "But Lord," I prayed, "didn't You call me here?"

God does provide where He calls, and He desires to care for His own, but I didn't know how far I could trust Him. I had not yet learned to pray the bold prayers of a confident child of God.

My prayer that day was a panicky cry for help. "Lord, You know I don't have these things," I said. "I've watched You provide spiritually for people in the churches where we've shared. Won't You please provide some practical things for me, too?"

The next week, at a church in hot, muggy Florida, another team member and I were placed in the home of an elderly lady. In my selfishness, I groaned. It was a small house, broken down a bit. I figured the lady must be poor and we'd have a rough week there.

But once inside, I was surprised. Her home was comfortable and cheerful—just like her. I loved her lacy curtains and the flowers on her table. "From the garden out back," she said. She offered us a glass of cool water and led us to the room where we would stay for the week.

Standing in the doorway of our room, my mouth opened in surprise. Then my lip quivered and I burst into tears.

There, on each of our beds, was a lovely gift basket to welcome us. I smiled at her and turned to examine the contents as she left to prepare our dinner.

Absolutely *everything* I'd prayed for filled that basket— and not just in small, sample sizes! This dear, sweet woman of God thought of everything a young girl might need or want. The personal supplies were there, the thank-you notes, and even chocolates (which I hadn't thought to ask for but sure did appreciate)!

And there was more. In the bottom of the basket was a twenty-dollar bill in an envelope for "whatever else you need."

I bowed my head, wiping away tears, as I confessed my lack of faith.

"Oh Father God, You are so good to me," I prayed. "I've never had to trust You this way before. Thank You for Your goodness. Thank You for Your faithfulness."

Then I jumped up from the bed and ran to tell the lady about my prayer and how God had used her to be my miraculous answer.

I've long since forgotten her name but never her kindness, and God knows her name. But I recognized this was far more than a gift from a caring old woman. The basket showed God loved and heard me. He cared about my needs. The gift was ultimately from Him, as are all good gifts (James 1:17).

God provided in a way that clearly reminded me I was not forgotten. He saw my service, heard my prayer, and proved Himself faithful and true. Asking for "bread," my Father did not give me a "stone" (Matthew 7:9).

In time, I learned to place my confidence in Him for all things. In the forty years to follow, serving with Life Action Ministries and in several other ministries including one with my husband, Bob, God continued to meet needs. But I still point back to that simple basket—the "Faithfulness Basket"— as the foundation of my understanding that God will always faithfully provide for His beloved children.

With maturity, I learned to trust Him as Paul did (Philippians 4:11–12), in times of want and times of abundance, knowing that His sovereign plan may sometimes lead through suffering but always for our ultimate good and His glory.

27

HE CALLS ME FRIEND

KIMBERLY DAVIDSON

Every spring I leave the raindrops and clouds of Oregon and head east to visit Mom and Dad. I joyfully anticipate the trip because it's the one time of year that I get to spend quality, girlfriend time with my mother. One of our favorite things to do is to shop—and shop a lot!

I inherited the shopping gene from my mother; however, I believe this gene is coded in almost every woman's DNA. I admit wholeheartedly I am one of those women whose blood pulses and heart soars as she nears the arches of a mall. Ironically, science has finally discovered what women have known all along: shopping for new clothes and shoes makes you feel good!

On this particular day we headed east to scavenge through our favorite collection of shops. The day couldn't have been more perfect, a warm and sunny seventy-eight degrees. My budget didn't allow me the luxury of purchasing much from this particular shopping center. My objective: find the best bargains.

Bursting through the door, I scanned the room. *There's the sale section! I may find that buried treasure among all those stacked and smashed clothes. Get out of my way!*

Disappointment, once again, dampened my mood. This was the third store . . . no prize. I located the two or three chairs set aside for the shoppers' impatient and bored companions. In my case, it was where the losers of the "sale" hunt sit waiting for those who are still foraging.

My eyes were drawn to a display. *What adorable Capri pants! And in my favorite colors: fuchsia, turquoise, and lime green.* These attractive pants had *really* caught my attention. I was envisioning how great they would look on me. *I think I'd look pretty cute! I wonder what they cost? I'm afraid to look.* Cautiously, I wandered over to the display and pulled out the price tag. *I knew it. No way!*

I reclaimed my seat but still couldn't take my eyes off those adorable pants. I started talking to myself and, in fun, said, *Maybe I'll tell Hubbie that God wanted me to have those pants!* I laughed to myself. *Like he'd believe that one!*

Then I asked my Friend, God, "Heavenly Father, how would I know if You wanted me to have those pants?" Of course, I didn't get an audible answer, so I continued my conversation with Him.

"Well, it would have to be some kind of miracle . . . like if my mother offered to buy them for me. Tee-hee."

That would be quite funny because as soon as I graduated from college (some thirty years before) and was able to support myself, my mother had never taken me clothes shopping on her dime. And I've never expected her to.

No more than thirty seconds went by when my mother came over and asked, "Did you see anything you liked?"

Whining, I replied, "I saw a lot of things I liked, especially those Capri pants." I pointed to them. "But I can't afford them."

It was as if the sky opened and my Best Friend's voice broke through. "I'll buy them for you if you want them."

The voice was my mother's. I almost fell off the chair but instead shot like a rocket over to the section with "my" Capri pants. *I must hurry before Mom and God both change their minds!*

Whoever said that God doesn't give us the desires of our heart and doesn't want to be part of our fun and joy was surely misguided. "Be delighted with the Lord. Then he will give you all your heart's desires" (Psalm 37:4 TLB). Not only does God want to bless us, but His very nature is to be a friend to us. He loves us with a perfect love and reaches down to us when we have nothing to offer in return . . . except our own love and friendship.

In the book of James we read that Abraham believed God, and he was called "the *friend* of God" (James 2:23). Jesus called His disciples friends. He said He would tell them things that His own Father had revealed because they were His friends.

If you think getting an unexpected pair of Capri pants is incredible, even a bit unbelievable, how about the ability to chat with God on a daily, minute-by-minute basis? We can ask Him for anything and share anything with Him as we would our Best Friend! He longs to hear from us. It doesn't mean we will always get what we ask for, but talking with God strengthens our relationship with Him. It's like walking into a major company and asking to speak directly to the CEO, and the secretary responds, "He'd be delighted!"

Spending time with God grew my faith, which is directly related to experiencing God as my Father, Provider, Healer, Counselor . . . and Friend. We each stand at an exciting door of opportunity to know God more intimately every time we believe Him for something in our lives, whether it's for a pair of Capri pants or the check for our mortgage. I can say, "I am a friend of God's! We even go shopping together!"

28

DIVINE DEBRIS

JEN MILLER

Nineteen and pedal-heavy, I raced my beat-up Pinto through the blue-collar lunch crowd traveling the congested streets of Dallas's east side. Between school and work, I was always short of time.

I was alone in life except for my sister, who lived nearby. She'd escaped our dad's ill clutches two years prior, vowing never to return. We shared the same vow, the same horrid memories that we'd never escape, and the responsibility for making it on our own in an adult world shockingly new to us. We'd been held captive, isolated from the day-to-day gears of society, and had each leaped into adulthood without due preparation. It was sink or swim, and since my leap I had been exhaustively treading water.

I was late for work, again.

My job at the prestigious six-story Texas State Bank kept me in the bowels of the building doing the filing—menial work for equally menial pay, for which I was quite grateful. I couldn't afford to lose my job; I was totally on my own and barely staying afloat.

I was attending college classes each morning and working every afternoon in an effort to make something of myself while striving to support myself. I'd always longed to be a teacher, hoping to make a difference in the life of at least one child who suffered silently at home, as my sister and I had through our growing-up years.

Merging into the vehicular mass moving south on I-635, my prayers persisted, as heavily as my foot bearing down on the gas, that I'd make it to work on time. I couldn't be late, for fear I'd be fired. *What would I do then? What would become of me?* My thoughts sped with my sky-blue Pinto. My sister didn't have the means to support me while I looked for another job. She could barely meet her own needs for survival.

Glancing between the side and rearview mirrors before attempting to squeeze into the left lane, fear struck and stunned me like a Taser. The red and blue lights flashing behind me, drawing quickly toward my dented bumper, were unmistakably flagging *me* down.

My heart, shocked into rapid awareness, plummeted heavy into my stomach as I gingerly steered my way to the opposite side and slowed to a stop on LBJ's concrete shoulder. Drivers slowed as they passed, and I could feel their scolding glances, as though I'd been summoned before them as jurors of the Supreme Court of Vehicular Justice.

The officer grew larger in my side-view mirror. It was clear that he was deftly trained to approach one inch from dirtying his clean and crisply pressed pant leg on a dusty door frame. My own mud-splattered car announced to the jurors-in-passing that I was not only a negligent driver but lazy in my responsibility toward car care.

I knew the drill. I was already reaching for my wallet when his six-foot frame swallowed me from the piercing Texas sun, made all the hotter by my shame and the searing truth that I had, indeed, been speeding and would, indeed, be late for work. The only coolness his shadow offered was in his law-enforcing demeanor. Hands on his menacingly wide and weighted black belt, at my eye level, he asked, "Ma'am, do you know how fast you were driving?"

The damage was twenty dollars—a hefty penalty for the poor. It was a lot of money for a college student making her way in the world alone, and spare change was nonexistent.

It was to be paid by May 13 "or appear before the court at 10:00 a.m." There was no misinterpreting the yellow carbon copy he handed me while reprimanding, "Slow down and be safe." The sound of passing citizens was redolent of the jurors' whispered verdict: "Guilty as charged! Off with her head!"

As the days languished long toward May 13, while my bank account continued to stall in the red, it became apparent to me that I'd be standing before a judge come that judgment day. There simply was no extra twenty dollars. I hadn't even had enough spare change in those three weeks to collect in a stay-out-of-jail jar.

I was terrified.

Early on the 13th, debilitating thoughts of an iron lock-down plagued my naiveté. I had two hours to find twenty dollars, and yet I knew that was an impossibility. I just didn't have it, and I knew my sister didn't, either. I was clammy with the certainty that "The Judge" would be mandating my future now. And I was positive that a punitive punishment would be pronounced unforgiving through the criminal justice system.

Every shallow breath was a pleading prayer for God's divine intervention as I drove—with due respect to driving decrees—across the twenty miles to the courthouse. The little yellow slip specifying the address rode shotgun on the seat next to me. It had held my thoughts prisoner through the interminable days, glaring accusingly at me from the top of my third- or fourth-hand chest of drawers wherever I situated myself in my dorm bedroom.

"Please help me, God, . . ." I pleaded aloud as I pulled into the courthouse parking lot at 9:50 a.m. My prayers continued fervently as I parked directly in front of the wide double doors over which was inscribed, "In God we trust." Nevertheless, I felt panicked. "Please help me, God. I need twenty dollars. Please . . . I need a miracle!"

Fevered with frenzy by 9:54, I desperately looked around through blurry eyes, as though God might suddenly appear in person and I'd miss Him.

I fought back tears as the full weight of my certain incarceration settled in me, and I slumped in my seat like dead weight, defeated.

The clutter on my floorboard testified against me in upstanding car care. There was a good three inches of refuse riding on the floor in front of the passenger seat: wadded napkins smeared and spotted with mustard and dollar store lipstick, a pair of crushed soda cups, a set of old class notes stamped with a dirty shoe print . . . . That was only the top layer visible through my tears. The debris had quietly accumulated for months. There never seemed to be enough time for car care between the need to get to class, get to work, and get some sleep.

I swallowed hard against the growing lump that had settled deep in my throat and cried, "Father, what am I going to do? Please help me!"

Look on the floor, He seemed to respond.

What? I was taken aback by the thought.

Desperate, I swiped at the tears to clear my vision then stretched myself across the tattered vinyl console to reach the passenger floorboard. Apparently He was seeing something I'd missed.

I began to rearrange and order the rubbish. Tissues and napkins to the right, school papers to the passenger seat (temporarily hiding the yellow ticket), paper cups and plastic lids to the left . . . . My floorboard had become a convenient burial ground for the discarded as I'd driven between school, work, the grocery store, and my shared room.

The semblance of order I'd created uncovered the bottom layer: several faded grocery store receipts, a broken pencil, a collection of balled-up silver gum wrappers, and a waste of used Texas State Bank envelopes from which I had pulled the meager cash rendered from my weekly paychecks.

I looked closer and blinked a couple of times at an envelope that stood out, strangely crisp and clean among its trashy neighbors. It looked brighter and ill out of place, though it had been buried at the bottom for months.

Open it, He prompted.

A flash of hope sparked in me as I reached for the envelope, but that glimmer was quickly dimmed by the sound slap of common sense that followed. The envelope would be just as empty as it had been when I'd removed its contents months ago; "Oh, ye of little faith." The heap of rubbish I'd rearranged to locate my dirty, gray-carpeted floorboard in search of a miracle suggested I'd find only disappointment.

I peeled back the tightly tucked-in flap while pulling myself upright. The center edge of a government-issued greenback blinked at me. I caught my breath and blinked back in disbelief, gaping at the green edging. In that moment, at the literal hour of my need, I once again wavered between faith and setting myself up for disappointment and defeat. Perhaps it was a one or five inside. But maybe . . . .

Hope wedged in to stand with doubt where desperation had resided only four minutes prior. The time was 9:58 when I slowly withdraw a crisp new bill from the crisp new envelope—and gasped.

What?! A twenty? How . . . ?

Questions can't be answered of miracles, I knew. There are no logical explanations, only divine interceding that renews our faith in God and settles for us once again that He knows, He sees, and He hears our needs.

A deluge of astonishment hit me as I stared full on at President Andrew Jackson, flanked on the right by a wide-winged eagle and in three corners the large federal font bearing the number *20*.

A tide of relief and gratitude flowed in the wake as I hugged them all close to my heart—the eagle, the seventh president, my joy and amazement, and my Father.

"Thank You, thank You, thank You . . . ." I whispered to Him. He had been riding shotgun with me all along.

29

A MOUTH FULL OF MIRACLES

TINA SAMPLES

He moaned as his grabbed his face. "It really hurts, Mama." I looked deep in his mouth, at every tooth, and around his gums, but I couldn't see anything. "I'm sorry, I know we need a dentist." I pulled him close and dug my nose into his soft brown hair. A waft of apple shampoo floated through my nostrils.

We'd just moved from Texas to Colorado and as a pastor's family of a small church made little money and had no health insurance. "Hold on—soon," my husband encouraged.

He was right, our insurance came through, and I couldn't make the dentist appointments fast enough.

"All four of you?" the attendant asked.

"Yes, ma'am—all four of us."

We looked rather comical, sitting there in a row. After a full investigation of our teeth, the doctor revealed the results.

"Well, you all need your teeth cleaned, we need to fill a few cavities, but other than that you look good—except for this guy here," he said, pointing to my youngest son. "He needs quite a bit of work and a specialist to do it."

I couldn't believe it. I felt horrible for waiting. I didn't waste any time in calling our insurance to find a pediatric dentist. I was filled with hope and thankfulness for the dental care. However, it didn't take long for my newfound hope to sour my stomach.

The insurance company shared that all the pediatric dentists in our area had pulled out of the program. "You mean there are no pediatric dentists in this area who take our insurance?"

"That's right—no one in your area," she said.

"How far away is the closest one?" I asked, hoping Wyoming would be a prospect.

After she mentioned a location several states away, I melted in grief. A large lump formed in the center of my throat, and tears welled in my eyes. I hung up the phone feeling defeated and beaten. I couldn't contain the tears any longer. I cried and prayed, "God, what are we going to do?"

I spent the next week flipping through the phone book. I called one pediatric dentist after another and asked if they would take payments—all of them said no. It didn't matter what kind of situation we were in, everyone needed the money up front. I was completely and utterly exhausted from trying.

After a while, I finally found someone willing to allow us to pay five hundred dollars up front—five hundred dollars we didn't have.

"Don't worry—we'll get it from somewhere," my husband consoled.

The date for the dentist was set. "Next week, son," I shared. "It won't be much longer."

I'm not sure why, but as the days passed leading up to the

appointment, I felt nervous and unsure. It is a feeling difficult to explain. Was I worried too much about the finances? My anxiety increased to an unhealthy level.

The day of my son's appointment, I awoke up with a knot in my stomach—as if I were the one needing the dentist. I rallied the kids, fed them breakfast, and packed their lunches.

Still uneasy about the day, I leaned down and looked deep into my son's blue eyes. "Hey—you go to school and I'll come get you and take you to the dentist, but if I don't come, it means you don't have an appointment today, okay?" He stared back at me, releasing a boyish grin.

"Okay, Mama." His smile always melted my heart.

I said my good-byes then made a beeline to the phone and phonebook. I had to search a little to find the dentist's office, but I called right away to cancel the appointment. "What is wrong with you, Tina?" I said while dialing the number. My spirit moved, and I knew I just couldn't take my son there.

While canceling my appointment with the one dentist office, my eyes fell upon an advertisement on the other side of the page of the phone book. In big bold letters it read, The Tooth Zone. I hung up from cancelling one appointment and immediately dialed the other office to inquire about their payments.

I shared my predicament with the woman taking the appointments. She assured, "Don't worry—we allow you to pay." Two days later, my son had an appointment.

The room was draped in vibrant colors. I couldn't get over how kid-friendly it was. Kids were running all over the place.

The waiting room held a huge gym in the center, spiraling up to the ceiling. Kids could climb to the top and go down a slide that opened up like a big mouth at the bottom. Video games were tucked in the back—all free for the kids to play. A coffee station and elegant waiting area for parents adorned the front lobby. I knew this was going to be an extremely expensive place. "Help us, Lord," was all I could pray.

The wait wasn't long, and they called my son back. My first impression of the doctor was complete shock. He was dressed in Bermuda shorts, flip-flops, and a very loud Hawaiian shirt. The entire back area was splashed in fun, energetic colors with lively music playing in the background. I was in awe of its creativity.

The doctor introduced himself, and I told him about my son's teeth. During our conversation, I shared we didn't have dental insurance and asked if they allowed others to make payments. He didn't respond to my question but turned and asked me several. He wanted to know quite a bit about my husband, what he did, our family, and how long we'd lived in Colorado.

At the closing, he said, "We'll get some X-rays, and I'll take a look. Don't worry, the ladies out front will get you settled."

My heart beat a million times faster than it should have. My stomach churned, and I felt nauseated. Just thinking about the bill caused my head to spin. I didn't want to hear it—I couldn't think of it. I kept praying, "God, what if they ask for an amount we don't have?" But I knew *any* amount they asked for would be something we didn't have.

I continued to fill out the dreaded paper work. I felt that if I took my time, then perhaps it would make things a little easier. After a little time of working on the forms, I felt a gentle tap on my shoulder. Startled, I jumped and looked up. The doctor smiled and motioned by jerking his head to the side to come with him.

I fearfully followed. He led me to a room with a conference table and chairs. He sat and asked me to sit, too. My forehead creased as concern draped my face.

"We've looked at your son's X-rays and teeth. He is going to need quite a bit of work." He pushed a piece of paper across the table and began sharing about the extensive work my son needed.

Despair floated midair from the large sigh I released. My heart sank as I looked at the dollar sign on the page. I'm sure he could see the anguish on my face. *How will we ever pay for this, Lord?* I silently prayed. We didn't have two hundred dollars, much less two thousand!

A silent pause filled the room, and thick emotion hung in the air. I couldn't speak. I sat in silence trying to hold back the tears.

"Mrs. Samples?"

I looked up and our eyes met.

"We're going to fix your son's teeth, but we won't charge you."

My sad, soppy eyes lifted in confusion.

"You see, what you didn't know is that I have a ministry to pastors' families. Every six months we close the doors and open it just for pastors' kids. I take care of their teeth free of charge."

I couldn't breathe, speak, or move. Large tears fell on the table as the doctor pushed a box of tissues my way.

"That's why I brought you in here," he comforted.

Elated and overwhelmed with God's love, broken speech found its way from my lips. "You . . . have . . . no idea . . . how close I came to going to someone else this week."

I couldn't thank him enough for such a generous act of kindness and love. It was a miracle. The uneasiness in my stomach was the Holy Spirit directing me. Before my eyes fell upon the ad in the phone book, I hadn't even heard of such a place. I was grasping, searching, and praying for God to direct me to the right dentist. God did the rest.

My son went through several months of dental work costing several thousands of dollars. My son and I relished the times when we could see the dentist.

Six months later we made our way back to the office. The atmosphere gleamed of kids running around, laughter, and fellowship. It didn't feel like a dentist's office. A sweet and fresh spirit lingered in the air.

Dr. Baker charged through the doors, smiled vigorously, clapped his hands together, and bellowed, "Oh yeah! Pastors' day!"

30

FISHES AND LOAVES . . . AND SPAGHETTI

TRACY CRUMP

There is a lad here, which hath five barley loaves,
and two small fishes: but what are they among so many?

JOHN 6:9 KJV

My son Jeremy tapped a gavel on the table. "I call this meeting to order."

The roomful of 4-Hers quieted as the children, well-versed in the proper conduct of a business meeting, prepared to give their various committee reports.

After the minutes and treasurer's report, I was asked to take the floor. "I'm sure most of you know Kenny and Kelly Johnson in the Explorers 4-H Club. I just found out that their dad, James, suffered a major heart attack a few days ago and had emergency surgery. Worse still, doctors found another problem that will require a second operation."

In as simple terms as possible, I explained the abdominal aortic aneurysm, a ballooning of the largest artery in the body, that physicians discovered during James's bypass. As a former nurse, I knew it left untreated was like a ticking time bomb. Eventually it will rupture and cost the patient his life.

"The doctors said Mr. Johnson will have to recover from his first surgery before they can operate for the aneurysm. But there's one more problem." I hesitated. "The Johnsons don't have any insurance." I explained that Mr. Johnson had just taken a new job that would pay better and finally provide insurance for his family. "He was within three days of being eligible for his company's insurance benefits when he had the heart attack."

The children and their moms sat silent as they absorbed this last bit of information.

"I know his family would appreciate our prayers."

As soon as I sat down, ten-year-old Aaron rose. "I would like to make a motion."

All eyes were upon him. "I move that we do a fund-raiser for the Johnsons."

How sweet, but I really don't have time for a monumental undertaking such as that. Besides, the Johnsons need the money now. Springtime always seemed so busy, and our 4-H calendar was already packed. I looked around the room and could tell the other mothers were thinking the same thing, but . . . I looked again. The children's eyes were shining.

Finally we agreed to pray about it, and I was assigned to ask the Johnsons for permission to conduct a benefit in their name if we elected to do it. The meeting adjourned, and we went on with our scheduled program.

At the next meeting, I could sense excitement in the air. Everyone talked at once, and the wheels had obviously been turning.

"Mr. Johnson is improving from his first surgery," I said, commanding everyone's attention, "and his wife said they would appreciate anything we could do to help them. Because of their insurance status, the hospital requires a five-hundred-dollar deposit. The surgeon insists on payment for the first surgery before he will consider a surgery date to repair the aneurysm. The cardiologist is asking for money, too, and they simply don't have it."

"Then we'd better get moving. Why don't we rent a booth at May Fair and sell baked goods?"

"How about a spaghetti supper?"

"Why not both?"

And these were the mothers talking.

Things happened so quickly, I could hardly keep up. Four moms put their lives on hold as they raced to help a family in distress. The phone lines burned between our homes. May Fair organizers told us it would cost one hundred dollars to rent a craft fair booth then gave us the booth at no charge because "it's for a benefit." The town paper agreed to advertise the fund-raisers at no cost.

One mom took it upon herself to cart her brood of five around to different businesses in our small town asking for donations of items to raffle. Within two hours she had ten items, ice to chill the bottled water we planned to sell, and an offer from a printing company to print raffle and spaghetti supper tickets plus signs for our baked goods booth—all free of charge. My head was spinning after she called to tell me of her bonanza. By that point, it was evident that God's hand was on the project.

Donations of baked goods poured in on the day of May Fair. One couple cooked homemade sausage and biscuits, arranged them in a pretty basket, and walked around to the other booths selling them. An out-of-town vendor heard of the benefit and donated one of her crafts to add to the raffle items. By the end of the day, we had made more than six hundred dollars—on baked goods and one-dollar raffle tickets.

The spaghetti supper proved even more incredible. A teen 4-Her contributed two hundred home-cooked rolls that rivaled those from a popular restaurant chain. A friend, whose husband worked for a food distributor, donated spaghetti sauce complete with meat, salad dressing, and even butter. People baked cakes and pies to sell at the dinner. That only left us paper products, pasta, and bagged salad to purchase, and we were all set.

The dinner went off without a hitch. After dishing our last plate of spaghetti that evening, we tallied up the number of meal tickets redeemed and calculated we had made around four hundred dollars, maybe five hundred total with the additional raffle tickets sold. But after counting the money, we found we had almost eleven hundred dollars! Everyone was flabbergasted. Just like the fishes and loaves, God had multiplied our feeble efforts to provide for someone in need.

When all was said and done, the James Johnson Benefit accumulated more than twenty-one hundred dollars—not a grand sum, perhaps, and certainly not enough to pay for open heart surgery, but it was more than we ever dreamed of making. We sent a five-hundred-dollar deposit to the hospital and split the balance between the two doctors, wondering where the Johnsons would get the rest of the money for surgery. When the cardiac surgeon heard about the benefit, however, he told Mrs. Johnson, "If you have that kind of backing from the community, I'm not worried about getting my fee."

Mr. Johnson had a successful aneurysm surgery and recovered quickly to return home to his family. Just as importantly, a group of children and their moms learned a lesson about stepping out on faith and trusting God for a miracle.

31

HIS ANSWER IN THE STORM

KATHLEEN KOHLER

"I don't know how we'll heat the house next winter," my husband, Loren, said one spring day. Our ever-shrinking wood supply, the only source of heat, had us both very worried.

Three years earlier our family of five had packed up and moved from our cramped home in the Seattle area suburbs. We rented a two-story cedar home on eight acres in the heart of the Cascade Mountains. With visions of Daniel Boone and Grizzly Adams, our boys, Ben age thirteen and Joe age twelve, along with their eight-year-old sister, Bethany, couldn't wait to trade life in town for a real wilderness adventure.

Homesteaded in the 1920s by the owner's grandmother, the fully modernized house boasted electric lights and indoor plumbing. The one drawback, the house was located twelve miles beyond public power and phone lines. However, a large propane generator, housed in an outbuilding on the property, served to power lights and a washing machine.

One-hundred-and-fifty-foot evergreens covered the acreage, which bordered the Mount Baker Snoqualmie National Forest. Douglas fir, Pacific hemlock, and western red cedar, some with trunks eight feet in diameter, stood like sentries twenty yards from our front door. Yet the landlord did not allow us to cut any timber from the property. He wanted his childhood home to remain as pristine as he remembered, where as a boy he'd climbed trees and ran in the woods.

Snowfall could blow in as early as October and stay until May. A wood cookstove and fireplace kept our home toasty warm during the coldest months of the year. Every year, when the winter snows finally melted, the firewood cutting season began.

During previous summers, we bought permits and scavenged wood from abandoned logging sites on national forest lands. This year, however, the forestry service had closed many of the areas and blocked off the roads. Most of the spots still open to cut firewood were on steep mountain slopes a far distance from where we could park our truck. And much of the wood available had rotted.

With the cost of firewood beyond our budget, we turned to the Lord for a solution to our problem. Our family gathered in the living room. Loren prayed, "Lord, You know we need wood to heat the house next winter. Please show us what to do."

Several weeks passed and we wondered how God would answer our prayer, until one spring night. With everyone tucked in and asleep, remnants of the WWII movie we'd watched before bed roared into my dreams. P-51 fighter planes barreled through the sky over our house. I threw my arm over my sleeping husband and screamed into the dark, "Watch out! They're going to hit us."

Jolted awake, Loren and I lay in the darkened room and listened to a storm rage outside. The wind screamed like a cougar between the granite face of Long Mountain and our house. Snaps and crashing sounds just outside our bedroom window kept us on edge.

"I hope none of the trees come down on the house," I said.

Our hearts pounded when we heard a sudden violent cracking. Several loud thuds shook the earth beneath us. "How close do you think that is?" I said as we huddled together under the covers.

Loren pulled me closer. "We'll find out in the morning."

We drifted in and out of an uneasy sleep the remainder of the night, wondering what destruction we'd find the next day.

The boys galloped down the stairs the next morning. "Did you hear the big storm last night?" Ben asked.

Joe grabbed his jacket from inside the closet. "Come on, Ben. Let's go see if our tree fort's okay."

"Wait," I said as I flipped an egg in the iron skillet. I pointed to their places at the table. "After breakfast."

Already seated, Loren swallowed a sip of coffee from a blue mug. "We'll go out together. There's sure to be broken limbs dangling from treetops. Could be dangerous."

When we emerged from the safety of the house, huge branches lay scattered across the front yard. We whispered a prayer of thanks that none of the mammoth trees had slammed into our house.

We jogged down our long driveway and explored farther into the woods.

Ben and Joe raced on ahead of us. "Wow."

"Mom, Dad, Bethany, come see," Ben shouted.

"Be careful," I called after them as we ran to catch up.

Standing behind the boys, we couldn't believe what we saw. Directly in the center of a wide stand of evergreens, three monster trees lay like matchsticks on the ground. We stared at deep craters in the earth left by the root balls when the trees toppled over.

Loren shook his head. "I've seen trees fall over before, but never anything this big."

A short path off the driveway, wide enough for our truck, ended right where the giants rested. It was as if God's finger reached beneath the night storm clouds, stirred the air, and tipped over those towering giants.

"Kids, there's our winter firewood," Loren said. "God's answer to our prayers."

Since our landlord allowed us to use blown-down trees for firewood, Loren ran up the driveway and drove back with the truck. Revving up the chainsaw, he began cutting up the logs. Ben grabbed a maul and wedge to split the rounds. We worked together like a relay team as we loaded the wood into the truck, then drove to the woodshed by the house and dumped it out. Joe and I chopped pieces to fit the woodstove and fireplace. Bethany, along with the rest of us, stacked the winter fuel supply in the woodshed.

So often when I pray for the Lord's help, I struggle to bring about the answer myself. Standing in front of the shed, I surveyed row after row of wood piled high to the rafters and realized God doesn't need my help. He only desires we ask and watch to see what He in His mighty power will do. From a year's supply of firewood, I learned God provides in ways I can't even dream of.

32

TRAVELING LAPTOP

SHIRLEY CORDER

"I can't go on long leave and continue to write!" I said to my husband. He'd just applied for three months' leave and planned for us to go overseas to the UK as well as visit various places in our home country of South Africa. "I'm just beginning to make progress with my writing. There's no way I can manage three months away from the computer."

"Surely there must be a way around this." Rob frowned. "Other writers travel. They go all over the world, but they don't stop writing."

"They have laptops." I ran my hands through my hair. "Oh, maybe I should just give up. It's not as if I'm famous or have a contract or anything."

"No, but you won't get a contract if you give up. You're right. You can't take a three-month break from writing. We'll have to get you a laptop."

"Oh yeah, right! We're going to go overseas, travel around South Africa, *and* buy a laptop? We don't have that sort of money."

"Well then, we'll pray for one," my pastor husband said. "We need this leave. And you need a laptop. We'll make a plan."

That night I sat at my computer and caught up on e-mails. I kept thinking about the laptop. That would be the answer, but it would take a miracle. We couldn't afford to buy one. They cost much more in those days than they do today, plus we lived in South Africa where technology is extremely expensive. I wrote to my online editing group, sending them an article to critique for me. We had been together for some years, and we were good friends, despite the fact that most of us had never met. Ruth was in another part of South Africa, Elaine was in England, and the other two were in different states of America. We often shared updates and needs with one another.

On impulse, I dashed off a note to them, telling of my predicament. "I can't see how I can carry on writing like this," I typed. "Every time I start to get into a routine, we go away and I don't have the computer." I hit Send, closed the computer, and went to bed.

The next morning, I padded through to the computer in my jammies, breakfast bowl in hand. I liked to check e-mails before my shower. I glanced through the posts, answering some, deleting some, and checking some to reread later. Suddenly my fingers paused. Jan, one of the two Americans in my group, had written to say she had an extra laptop. The day before my e-mail, she had prayed for guidance who to give it to.

"Now I know!" she said. "It's meant for you. But I have no idea how to get it to you."

Three e-mails further down I came to an e-mail from the other American, Yvonne, sent a few hours prior to Jan's. "I want to donate X amount of dollars," she had written. "I realize it's nowhere near enough to get a laptop, but maybe it'll help."

The next day was Sunday, and I shared the story in church. "It's so exciting. I now have a laptop. All that's needed is to get it to South Africa." I laughed and sat down.

At the end of the service, a man came up to me.

"My daughter lives in New York City," he said. "She's coming here next week on vacation. If you can find a way to get it to her, she will bring it out for you."

I could scarcely believe it. I had only asked my critique group and the congregation for prayer. Yet it was as if the plan had been prearranged, and the final cogs were now falling into place. A few e-mails later, and it was all set up. To courier the laptop from Jan's home to New York City would cost almost the exact amount Yvonne had offered. Why was I surprised?

I waited nervously to hear the machine had arrived safely at its first destination. For the next week, e-mails flew back and forth through the cyber waves. Every day brought a fresh dose of panic. We have a different voltage system from America. What if the laptop didn't boot up? Would I need a different transformer? What if the machine got broken on the way? What if it was stolen? I wondered what I would say to my friends if, after all this, I didn't have a working laptop.

Six days after my initial e-mail to the group, I responded to a knock on the door. There stood the gentleman from our church. In his hands he held a black laptop case. "This is yours, I believe." He grinned as I stretched out my hands to receive it. It had really happened. I had a laptop, all the way from America.

I plugged it in and nervously flicked the switch. I watched it carefully in case it blew up because the current was wrong. What if nothing happened?

Nothing happened.

Then there was a flicker, and across the screen scrolled a message: "Hi. I come to you with lots of love from Jan." Tears streamed down my face as the machine completed booting up, and I gazed at the beautiful background photograph of Jan's home ranch in California.

Several months later, Rob and I left our home for a three-month vacation. It was difficult to know what to take, as it was winter for us but summer in the UK. We discussed how many books we should carry, and what to take to do on the plane. We debated what medication to pack in case we got ill. So many questions, but not once did either of us wonder about whether I should take my well-traveled laptop.

It journeyed around South Africa with me. It flew in the cabin of a jumbo passenger plane to London. I typed on it in bedrooms of guest houses and at the homes of friends. It sat on my lap on coaches and trains speeding through the countryside from England to Scotland and back.

I wrote articles and sent them to my group for critiques. I edited the text then submitted the articles to publications. In between, I did sightseeing and gathered more information and inspiration for further writing.

Yes, I was away from home for three months, but I didn't

have to give up my writing. It came with me. Today I am a multi-published writer, author of one book and contributing author to more than ten others. My writing didn't suffer, thanks to the generous teamwork of loving cyber friends, God's amazing grace, and my traveling laptop.

33

THE GOODNESS OF GOD

BEAU CORNERSTONE

Therefore take no thought, saying, What shall we eat?
or, What shall we drink? or, Wherewithal shall we be clothed?
(For after all these things do the Gentiles seek:) for your heavenly
Father knoweth that ye have need of all these things.
But seek ye first the kingdom of God, and his righteousness;
and all these things shall be added unto you.

MATTHEW 6:31–33 KJV

I was sixteen, and I'd moved to the city because there wasn't a senior high school in the country town my parents lived in. I was living by myself, renting a unit—juggling school, homework, and exams with keeping house, budgeting, and shopping.

Financially I was receiving a "living-away-from-home" government student allowance. It covered the rent, with about thirty dollars a week remaining for food, electricity, and everything else. It wasn't a lot of money at the time—but I came from a frugal family and, in spite of my youth, was good at budgeting, so usually I could make do on the allowance.

Graduation week loomed—the end of my secondary school training. God used that graduation week to teach me

194

an indelible lesson: He is Jehovah Jireh, our God who can be trusted to provide for all of our needs.

It began with a request from my teacher for everyone in our class to bring ten dollars for our graduation dinner in a week's time. I was secretly astonished—ten dollars for *one* meal? I cycled to the bank during lunchtime and paid for my graduation dinner that afternoon with just a flicker of concern—the power bill was due next week, too . . . .

I was in the habit of setting aside some money each week into a "bills purse," but sometimes my estimate of what a bill would be was an underestimate and the bills purse would need topping up from the food budget to pay a bill in full. This was one of those times; I needed to take another ten dollars out of the week's food budget.

By Saturday I "owed no man nothing," but I only had ten dollars left for food until my next student payment.

On Sunday I met up with Christians from the fellowship group I attended but told them nothing about the lean week ahead of me. As I dropped in an offering of one dollar from the ten dollars I had left, I told God I was sorry that it wasn't as much as I wanted to put in. Simultaneously the still, small voice reminded me of the widow's mite.

I went home and sorted out my pantry, trying to work out what I should buy for the week to make the most of the money I had left. I recall having a lot of flour in the cupboard but not a lot of anything else. I remember making damper for dinner that night and pancakes for breakfast the following morning.

When I rode my bike home from school that afternoon, I was surprised to find two cabbages and a bag of lemons on my front doorstep—an unexpected gift from my Italian landlord. I thanked God for His provision and made a concoction of fried cabbage and lemon juice battered in flour. I remember it tasted surprisingly nice although that might have been because I was hungry—I admit I've never made it since!

On Tuesday I came home from school and a gray-haired woman who lived in one of the other units came running up to me. I'd never really spoken to her because she always seemed to have a frown on her face. This time, however, she was smiling, and she handed me a packet wrapped in butcher paper. She explained that the butcher had given her a dozen sausages when she'd only asked for *half* a dozen—so she wanted me to have the extra six! I was overwhelmed with gratefulness toward both her and God. I ate half of the sausages for tea and took the rest to school for lunch next day.

On Wednesday evening I came home from school—intending to wash away my day and then go shopping for milk and Weetbix with my nine dollars. As I was about to leave for the shops, I heard a knock at the door. Two of the leaders from the fellowship group I attended were standing there with a laundry basket full of food! They had never given me food before, but apparently they'd been praying and God had laid it on their hearts to bring me a basket of food! The basket contained Weetbix and milk—and plenty of other things, too! I thanked them gratefully as I loaded everything into my pantry and went to bed with a full tummy, pondering on how amazing God was!

The following afternoon I arrived home from school to yet another surprise: not cabbages on my doorstep but two strangers sitting in a motorhome parked in my driveway. I wheeled my bike past them and unlocked my door. They both got out of the motorhome and approached me. They were youngish men, about in their twenties, and well dressed. I thought at first they must have been lost, except they called out to me and knew my name. They explained that they were my mum's second cousins. I hesitated for a moment then noticed that one had a Bible under his arm. The other was holding a family-sized tub of Kentucky Fried Chicken—and *that* was the deciding factor! I absolutely *loved* Kentucky Fried Chicken! It was a special treat for me, and the smell drifting out from the tub was tantalizing! We sat down and ate, and the whole time they were reading from the Bible and talking about past revivals and the Christian walk. Looking back, I *really* wish I'd listened more carefully to what they were saying, but at the time I was just stuffing my face with KFC! After I'd eaten to my heart's content, we prayed together. And then around nightfall they left. I put the leftover KFC into the fridge. I recall looking in the tub and noticing something unusual—the tub was still almost full of chicken, yet I knew I'd eaten about five pieces of chicken out of it. And they'd been eating, too . . . .

Friday came—the night of the graduation dinner. It was a fancy smorgasbord, eat-all-you-can dinner, and I made the most of it. I also remember filling up my pockets with short-bread biscuits as well! I pedaled home from the graduation dinner and reflected that I had made it through one of the leanest financial weeks in my teenage life, and not only did I *still* have nine dollars, but I also had heaps more food in the pantry and fridge than I had at the start of the week!

On Saturday my mum rang. I told her about the yummy graduation dinner (and glossed over the bit about being short of food money that week). Then I told her about her second cousins who had dropped in and visited me and their gift of KFC. Mum probed for details so I described their appearance and accents and the way they'd talked about the Bible. Mum grew really quiet then eventually told me that she didn't have any second cousins who matched the description of my visitors. After her words sunk in, I expected her to growl at me for letting strangers in, but instead she said maybe they were "angels unaware."

Even to this day when I reflect on that week, I think of how different things might have been if I'd pursued alternative "solutions" to my financial stress—solutions like asking a welfare agency for a food voucher or reaching for a credit card. Instead, that week God gave me a glimpse of His nature—His goodness, His provision (and His sense of humor!). The overall impact on my life has been a little like the rippling effect of tossing a pebble into water. At times when as a family work is short and we've needed a "top up" of food, I've been able to think back to the other times He's provided food for us and trust Him to provide for us again. I remember one time we prayed before going fishing for food. We not only caught enough fish to stock up our freezer, but we were able to give fish away to several other families as well!

Do angels eat KFC while studying the Bible with teenagers? Perhaps my visitors were only a couple of random travelers who somehow found out my name and favorite food and decided to drop in on me and hold a Bible study. To this day I still don't know. All I know is that, whoever they were, I've never forgotten God's supernatural provision that evening—indeed, His provision that entire week. It started out as a widow's mite . . . .

34

THE TREE

KRISTY HUSEBY

As he brushed the hair from his eyes, I glimpsed the familiar crinkle on his forehead that always appeared when Dad was upset.

Oh no—this can't be good, I thought.

We had all been summoned into the living room for the infamous "family meeting." From time to time we had these meetings, usually when one of us wanted to discuss things, like getting a dog or what we wanted to do on our vacation. Usually, these meetings were something I enjoyed, but I could tell this one was going to be different.

My father quickly got down to the matter at hand. "We need to decide, as a family, whether we will have a Christmas tree or presents this year. Our financial situation dictates that we won't be able to do both. I'm sorry it has to be this way."

I heard the sadness in his voice. He wanted it to be different, but it just wasn't. Life was like that sometimes.

I immediately thought, *Well, that's a no-brainer! I'll take a present, of course!*

But wait a minute, NO CHRISTMAS TREE? What would we do? Where would we put our presents? It wouldn't feel like Christmas without a tree. It's already hard enough celebrating

Christmas in the warm climate of California, and now we might be doing it without a tree as well!

In high school my dad had a life-changing encounter with Jesus Christ. It radically changed his life and his desires for the future. He chose to follow God wherever that might lead. His goal in life was never to make a lot of money but to serve the God he loved with his whole heart. Because of this we never lived with the expectation that we would have a whole lot of money, but I never felt poor, either. Sure, I usually got the "latest thing" about two years after it was the "latest thing," and it's not to say I liked it but I had kind of gotten used to the way things were.

My parents were always creative with our lack of money. One of our favorite family night activities was going to K-mart. We each had a dollar to spend however we wanted. I would stroll up and down the aisles looking at all the things I could buy. But I usually ended up with a big carton of malted milk balls. If I had any money left over, I would ask my sister if she wanted to pool our last coins together and buy something we could split. I loved seeing how far I could stretch that itty-bitty dollar.

We had to make other sacrifices due to our financial constraints along the way, as well, but we'd never had to face the choice of a present or a tree. This was a new one for all of us.

After quite a short conversation, it was unanimous. My siblings and I agreed that we would take presents over a Christmas tree any day!

So we immediately began to plan what our Christmas

would look like without a tree. We had always hung our stockings on our fireplace mantel. Why not put the presents around the fireplace? That would work! We could do without the tree, and our Christmas would still be memorable. Maybe even more . . . who knew?

Over the years when our family would struggle financially we were taught to tell God about it. The idea of ever telling anyone else that we were having a hard time was never an option. My dad made that very clear—we were going to trust God and that was that.

"Our God is big, He owns the cattle on a thousand hills, and He will take care of us."

I have had the amazing privilege of witnessing over and over throughout the years His incredible answers to prayer in our lives.

But I confess I never even thought to pray about a Christmas tree. Deep in my heart I wondered, *Isn't this Christmas tree a want, not a need? Starving people are in Africa, families are homeless, and children are being abused. God has so much more to be concerned about than my simple wish for a tree.*

Life went on its busy way, as it does at that time of the year, and the Christmas tree wish was lost in the plans of the season.

One bright sunny day, I was helping my mom decorate the house when the doorbell rang. I rushed to answer it and found a blue spruce standing at the door! I stood there gaping, speechless. Then the tree moved, and I saw one of our dearest friends standing behind it.

I pulled my jaw off the floor, found my voice, and yelled, "Mom, you're not going to believe this, but we have a Christmas tree at our door!"

Our friend carried it in and stood it on the floor of our living room. I followed him in a daze, my thoughts racing around in my head.

How did he know we needed a tree? Who told him? Why would God answer a prayer I hadn't even prayed?

But He did! And we were going to celebrate it. We put on some good old Christmas music, dug out the Christmas lights from storage, and hung our favorite ornaments on the tree. The tree itself was actually quite scraggly. It was a typical Charlie Brown Christmas tree. The branches were few and far between, but to me it was the most beautiful tree we had ever had!

Friends stopped by to visit during that holiday season and glimpsed our plain, ordinary tree standing tall in the corner of our living room. They might even have wondered why we would ever have paid money for such a tree as ours. But for me that tree was more than ordinary; it had the touch of the Eternal. It was holy ground. Because that is where I learned that my God wasn't just concerned about the important things of my life but the mundane, the ordinary.

That Christmas a young girl glimpsed a God who gives just because He *IS*. He is bigger than she could ever understand. He is greater than she could ever comprehend, and He loves more extravagantly than she will ever know.

As I think of that long-ago Christmas tree more than forty

years past, I'm reminded of another tree where God first demonstrated His extravagant love for me; a love that will not let me go, a love I cannot earn, a love that is timeless . . . .

PART 5

EVERYDAY
MIRACLES

35

HOPE IN THE WILDERNESS

JADE MAZARIN

Sometimes hope is all that we have. We find ourselves trudging through a wilderness of suffering, and the only thing that we can cling to is imagining more. Then there are moments along the journey when we feel stuck. The passage through feels more like a holding point in our lives, and we can't imagine feeling differently. But beneath it all, beneath the pain and sorrow, the sense of emptiness and fear, lies something deeper. There lies an opportunity. There exists an open door for a type of intimacy with God that is born only from such places. And in that place lies the fertile ground for redemptive light in the most fallen darkness.

When I began graduate school for my degree in counseling, little did I know that I was soon in for some of the most burdensome emotional experiences I had ever endured.

My arrival in Atlanta was accompanied by a deep sense of loneliness and isolation. I had left the comfort of college, with all its familiarity and close relationships, to enter a busy city of strangers and acquaintances. My first few months were also defined by a long and severe physical illness that only deepened my sense of longing for a "home." Despite healing from the sickness many months later, I felt drained by the experience and even more vulnerable to the pain of missing what I no longer had. I searched for a way to bring myself joy but could find nothing to comfort me within.

Slowly, severe depression settled through my heart, and I encountered a place of darkness that seemed all too easy to slip into. I felt aching emptiness every day. After several months, my depression led me into another aspect of inner pain—constant, severe anxiety. I couldn't explain the strange feelings I began to experience, and particularly the odd thoughts that came about all too naturally. The feelings were overwhelming. They seemed out of my control entirely, and despite my avid attempts to gain control over it, I could find neither an explanation nor any release. In fact, the more that I tried to gain control over this thing that felt so evil, the more badly I felt. *There is such a thing as evil*, I thought.

But as the months passed by, I felt God slowly leading me to consider His presence. I began to consider the power of God, His tender love for me, and the way He had touched my life in past events. A great thing happened when I stopped seeing the darkness as a place of evil. I saw the hope of God, and I began to consider that maybe, just maybe, it was possible, even in something so ugly, to find something remarkably beautiful. I focused on the Psalms and Isaiah, on verses of radical restoration and reliable hope. I prayed that while God got me through it, He would also use this for every good purpose that He could. So I surrendered. Even in my pain I told God I would follow Him as long as He walked in front and led me. Right afterward I randomly opened by Bible and my eyes settled on this verse: "He goes on ahead of his sheep and they follow him" (see John 10:4). *Hmm, thanks, Lord. You are with me,* I thought.

In faith that He would desire to do so, I prayed that He wouldn't let me experience this for nothing. Around that time, a quiet but strong thought rose up within me: *This is the preparation for the work He would have me do.* God then began teaching me how to see every moment (and they were constant) as an opportunity. I considered the beauty of my complete reliance on God, and I attempted to heed the quiet, small Voice within that nudged me to continue. When I experienced pain, I likened it to exercise and a time to build up my inner muscles. Of course I still had many moments of doubt. But I always came back to knowing—and this is so important—that God cared for my pain, deeply.

But while I surrendered and looked to His work in the pain, I never gave up on Him healing me of every negative emotion. Never. And I let Him know that I expected not just improvement but total renewal. I knew He could do it, and I knew that was His goal for my life.

The first few years I felt the tenderness and nearness of God rarely and in certain moments. But the more I studied His Word, shared my heart, and focused my eyes on Him, the more a gradual and quiet, yet noticeable, shift took place. I felt a gentle satisfaction in resting my gaze on Him. In fact I got so used to it that it became my sense of home. I also began feeling His kind, tangible presence. Every day. I no longer felt depressed. That aloneness that ached inside was being filled. I felt company. Deep, inner soul company. God knew it all—where I had come from, what I was still feeling, and where I would go. He also treated me with the attention that comes from a Father to His only daughter. I began to feel so close to Him I might as well have been His only child.

Yet oddly enough, even though I felt this communing with God, I still struggled with tormenting, distressing thoughts. Sometimes it was horribly burdensome. Then out of nowhere I had a clear picture in my head. It was an image of me, with my arms and hands held out, standing under the rain. I felt it was God sending His Spirit and His help down to me. And I didn't have to try to have peace anymore; I was just given it. I would bring up this picture anytime I needed hope. I never shared it with anyone. But I knew whenever I brought up this mental picture, that no matter how lost I felt or how long it had been, God could still give me my life back.

About five months later, something amazing happened. I had just come home from a long day of classes and constant anxiety. I got my mail, plopped down on the couch, and sighed. "Lord," I said, "I have put all of my faith in You. You just can't let me down." I looked down to my coffee table and grabbed a card from a friend of mine in North Carolina. I opened it and couldn't believe what was on the cover. It was a little girl with brown hair (my hair color), holding out her arms with her hands up as the clouds poured rain down on her. Then the caption below said, "Just when we think we will never smile again, life comes back." Eyes filling with tears, I put the card on my bureau where I could look at it all the time.

It has now been about five years since all of that happened, and I have the peace that I knew God would give me. Old feelings are still triggered occasionally, but God has used that to teach me how to pray over those old memories. He has also taught me how to do that with clients. I am now a board certified Christian counselor, and my favorite thing to do is help others grow intimacy with the same Father I found. I share pieces of this story whenever they need hope.

While I petitioned God only for healing, that was not the only thing I got. I found my health, yes. But I also became united with my Heavenly Father in a new way, and I get to take that with me. I feel Him today, tangibly, just as I started to years ago.

If you are suffering today, dear friend, know that the same investment, the same tenderness, the same incomparable compassion, and the same relentless hope that God had for me, He also has for you. You are His "only" child, too. Always know the depth of His heart for you, every moment of every day. Remember that "weeping may remain for a night, but rejoicing comes in the morning" (Psalm 30:5 NIV)—and God cannot help but cause it. There is more to this than you can see. Insist on it, as I did. And "The zeal of the LORD Almighty will accomplish this" (Isaiah 37:32 NIV).

36

MIRACLE IN THE MEN'S ROOM

TONI BABCOCK

Sometimes in the most mundane of circumstances, God appears to turn the monotonous into the miraculous. Never underestimate the power of the living God. Recall the Old Testament story when the sons of the prophets commenced to chop down trees near the Jordan River to build a new place to dwell? And how a man's borrowed ax head fell into the water, and the prophet Elisha threw in a stick and the iron floated (see 2 Kings 6:1–7). Well, here's *my* story . . . .

It's been said "what goes around comes around." I was about to test the tired cliché (literally) when I flushed my work keys down the toilet.

My day began like any other. I punched in, took the elevator to the third floor, loaded my yellow cleaning cart, and took an inventory of my supplies. Paper towels? Check. Clean rags? Check. Mop heads? Check. Disinfectant? Check. Cleanser? Check. Toilet bowl cleaner? Check. Glass cleaner? Check. Plastic bags? Check. Disposable gloves? Check. I proceeded to pull my cart out of the supply room and continued on, pushing past an open space to the trash room with my vacuum in tow. I stopped to snap on some disposable gloves and parked by a slop sink to fill my empty mop bucket, aiming a gray hose into the pail. After filling the bucket with fresh cleaning solution, I headed south with my cart to the lower level, dragging the vacuum behind. I had high hopes for a grand day.

The morning of "the incident" I was on restroom duty. It does have its quiet satisfaction. Like snapping open a clean trash bag to replace the bulging bags stuffed with damp paper towels or restoring mirrors to crystal clarity where drippy stains stared shamelessly before. And then . . . ah, yes . . . on to the toilets, with their sanitary issues to attend to. It's a dirty job, but somebody's got to do it. I know how good it feels to walk into a clean stall; now here is my time to pay it forward. Finally, the rhythmic swish and sway of my blue cotton mop as I walk backward, stepping and swinging all the way to the bathroom door where I mark my ceremonious waltz with a "Caution, Wet Floor" sign.

Now that *would* have been my regular routine, had I not been dislodged from my work keys in a most unceremonious way. I had entered into the men's room after knocking on the door to ensure it was empty. I replaced the trash bags and washed the sinks, mirrors, etc., then I had just entered a bathroom stall to clean the toilet. My thoughts turn somewhat into a blur at this point. I remember unlocking the toilet paper dispenser and, with my work keys in hand, reaching over to flush the toilet. I can still hear the sucking sound of a zealous flush, but worse than that, feeling the loss of my keys in an instant from the palm of my hand! I still see the gaping toilet bowl as my keys flew toward the vortex, and I watched in muted horror as they slipped into oblivion, in one dramatic surge down the black hole! They were gone! Oh no! What would my boss think?

So what does a frantic environmental services attendant (a.k.a. cleaning lady) do in such a terrible fix? Find the nearest maintenance man. Okay, I know that sounds pathetic, but maintenance men can work miracles, right? I was about to find out. I placed two pieces of masking tape over the toilet seat so no one would use it then ran to find a willing man. It was quite early in the morning, but I hoped not too early to locate one of the guys who could dutifully assist a damsel in distress. I found "Rick."

"You'll never get those keys back," Rick informed me point-blank (emphasis on "never").

What? I thought. *But you're the maintenance guy. You fix stuff!* I was struck speechless. Where had male chivalry gone? I figured the sight of a weak and helpless post-menopausal woman in a serious panic would pull the man strings at least a little bit, but instead I was faced with the uncomfortable perception that Rick sort of wished he were a million miles away. My spectacled eyes were pleading, but his gray-blue eyes were fixed in a faraway stare. He shook his head glumly to confirm the grim analysis.

Was I reading him wrong, or did he just not *want* to fish my keys out of the men's room toilet? Hmmmm. I felt a little spark of faith light within. "I can do all things through Christ who strengthens me" seemed to take over my thoughts. No more girly-girl excuses. No more theatrics. Time to get my "go girl" on. Don't get me wrong, Rick is actually a great guy, and God bless him, but I didn't need him for this. It was the Lord and me from here on out. Suddenly I was pumped and looking for the nearest coat hanger.

I left the maintenance guy for the nearest closet to find a metal hanger. Voilà! Metal hanger found in first-floor closet near the chapel. Hope was surging. I pulled it apart to fashion a long rod with a hook. I sprinted back down the stairs to the lower level and ran into the men's room. I stood near the stall and called upon the name of the Lord for good success. Show time. I ripped the tape off of the toilet seat and stuck the homemade hook way down into the yawn of the porcelain basin, twisting it gently. God is good! Something grabbed! Slowly I pulled up. I felt a dragging! A little farther . . . and . . . my keys! Praise the Lord!

A quick soak in some disinfectant and my keys were good to go. I was reminded once again that "our help is in the name of the LORD, who made heaven and earth" (Psalm 124:8 KJV). Thanks anyway, Rick.

37

GOD'S AMAZING GRACE

NANCY GIBBS

Every time an earnest prayer is uttered to God, He hears it in a concerned and loving way. The most elegant prayer doesn't get God's attention any quicker than the humblest of prayers whispered by His children. I discovered a great truth on a beautiful spring day many years ago. A few words spoken by the heart are as important to God as the longest plea for help.

As a young mother, I was confined to my home during the daytime hours. My twin sons, Brad and Chad, were four years old at the time, and we were anxiously expecting our third child. We owned only one car. My husband traveled during the day; therefore, I had no transportation. At times, I considered taking a job outside of the home, to enable us to purchase a second car. After considering the pros and cons, however, I chose to stay at home with my children for as long as possible. My husband, Roy, supported my decision wholeheartedly.

I ran the household errands and bought our groceries after Roy arrived home at night. This arrangement gave me a chance to get away from the daily responsibilities of motherhood and housework. It also afforded Roy the opportunity to spend quality time with our sons while I was away. To me, the situation was ideal, except for the worry of an unexpected emergency.

This particular spring day, when I was in the third trimester of my pregnancy, Brad broke his arm, as he sailed off the bunk beds in the boys' bedroom while holding on to the drapery cord. He discovered the hard way that Superman had a special talent, one that he himself didn't possess—he couldn't fly! When I reached his side, the sight of his arm alerted me to the dreaded emergency before me. I knew I had to get him to the hospital immediately.

How will I handle this? I wondered, as I picked Brad up and held him close to my heart. I grabbed the phone and dialed my father's telephone number at work. Normally, it was very difficult to reach him, so I was surprised when he answered my call on the first ring. He assured me that he would be there as quickly as possible. While we waited for him, I rocked Brad and sang continuously to the Savior. My off-key version of an old hymn calmed my little boy's fears and strengthened my faith.

The thought crossed my mind that Roy would be coming home to an empty house later that day. I knew he would be frightened if he came home to a note stating that we were at the hospital. Even though my pregnancy was going well, the doctor was still concerned that I might have a premature delivery.

How can I reach my husband? I wondered. Back then nobody had cell phones. I didn't want him to panic. In addition, Brad and I both needed Roy to be there with us. Chad was very upset, too. We needed to face this emergency situation together, as a family. *What if I go into labor?* I wondered. *I would definitely need him to be there.*

Almost immediately, my faith in God strengthened while I continued to sing to my son. I felt the unexplainable presence of God's amazing grace as I held Brad closely. I also felt the peace that passes understanding as I closed my eyes and humbly asked God to nudge my husband to call home.

"He'll be terrified, Lord," I whispered with my heart, as I continued to sing to Brad. "Please have him call home before Daddy gets here." Just as I lifted my head and opened my eyes, the telephone rang.

"Hello, Roy!" I shouted, knowing that God had answered my prayer, even before I heard my husband's voice on the other end of the line.

He had no idea why he had called, but he'd just had the feeling that something was wrong. When the thought crossed his mind that he was needed at home, he stopped at the next interstate exit and called long distance from a pay phone.

"Brad broke his arm," I cried. About that time, I heard my father's car pull up onto the driveway. "I need to go," I said. "Daddy is here to take us to the hospital. I'll meet you there. Please be careful driving," I begged.

Shortly after we got to the hospital, Roy met us in the emergency room. My heartfelt prayer for him to call before my father arrived had been answered just in the nick of time. Roy kept his cool and didn't panic while driving to the hospital. He knew that with God's help the situation was under control. Shortly after his arrival, X-rays were taken of Brad's badly broken arm. He was sedated to avoid shock and rushed into the operating room to have his arm set and put in a cast. Roy comforted Chad as I sat near them. His presence kept us both calm during the entire procedure.

When the nurses brought my precious little Superman back to his room, he was twirling the blades of a toy helicopter, which had been placed on his stomach. I rejoiced in the fact that God had been with us throughout the entire ordeal. I felt the touch of the Master's hand from the moment I began singing about His amazing grace until the time Brad was returned to us.

The power of prayer is the greatest force in the universe. My personal relationship with Jesus Christ gave me the instinct to pray without using elegant or formal words. I stated my need. He responded. Even though God knows our every need, it is His desire that we should seek His help in all situations. He's willing, able, and quick to respond to our every plea, when we earnestly call on Him.

Today, some thirty-five years later, I am grateful for the time that I was given to stay home with my children while they were young. Like in any typical household, there were several other emergencies, which I faced as they grew up. I knew without a doubt, however, that there was nothing that could happen to us that God and I couldn't handle together.

After my children became adults and moved away, I placed each of them in the Master's hands. With a great deal of God's amazing grace and the magnificent power of prayer, I have the faith that I can trust a loving God to watch over them, regardless of any situation they may encounter.

Because of His answered prayer many years ago, I have the assurance that God will stay by my side, hearing all of my heartfelt prayer requests. Not only will He hear my humblest pleas; His amazing grace will always be sufficient for me.

38

A SONG FROM HEAVEN

BOBBY BARBARA SMITH

In the last months of my mother's life, she would slip in and out of a world known only to her. When she was in "Her World," we would all try to reach her, to draw her back to us. But the pull from that other world was stronger, and so we lived for the clear days, when she was in ours.

On one such day, my mother drew me to her bedside and searched my face before she spoke.

"Mom came to me yesterday." I can tell you I was not prepared for the story mother shared, but I hung on every word, as she told of a visit from the other side.

"Mom was trying to teach me something. It was like a dream but more real." She struggled for the right words before continuing.

"I understood clearly what she was saying." Mother paused then looked deeply into my eyes.

"Mom sang an old song that she used to sing while she went about her work in the kitchen. I had forgotten that song. I wish I had the words."

I caught my breath then asked, "Do you know the name of the song?"

She couldn't remember the name, but she sang the chorus,

struggling to recall the words.

"Far away, beyond the starry night, where the love light never, never dies.

Gleameth a mansion, filled with delight, sweet happy home so bright."

As my mother sang, I sensed the importance of the song, wanting to remember as much as possible. Before I left, I promised to look for the words. I knew it would be a difficult task. I didn't have the title, and it was quite an old song.

My mother's birthday was fast approaching, and I knew that song would be the perfect gift. I searched old hymnals and asked friends, with no luck.

One day, as I listened to a "Swap-n-Shop" radio show, I decided to appeal to the good people of Arkansas. I called in and told them about my mother's desire to find the words to her mom's old song. I gave them what few words I had and offered to pay whatever was fair, for the words. I hung up thinking nothing would come of it. I was wrong!

Before the afternoon was done, I not only had the words to my mother's song; I had the music and a tape! A lovely family made the tape for me. They filled the rest of the tape with beautiful songs all about mothers. Another lady furnished a copy of the music and the words. Not one of those wonderful people would take a dime for the time or money spent. My heart was overcome with gratitude.

Oh, what a birthday that was! I popped that tape in Mother's player and watched as her face flooded with tears of joy.

"That's it! I can't believe you found it!" I shared with her about the wonderful people and how they gave freely with nothing but love.

"Mom, it was like a gift from heaven, the way I found those people and your song." She smiled and said, "It was. It was a gift from heaven."

Mother played her song so much that before long we both had it committed to memory. I had no way of knowing what an important role that song would play in the months to come.

Soon my mother slipped into "Her World," and nothing we could do would draw her back to ours. We knew the end was near.

Before Mother's health had failed, she had crocheted a beautiful afghan for all of her children except for my younger sister Donna. I recalled her asking what colors Donna liked, and I promised to find out, but when Mother became ill, we all forgot about the afghan—all, that is, except Mother.

There in her hospital bed, away in her world, she would sit for hours, working in a strained position on an imaginary afghan. I would beg her to lay down her "yarn" and rest, but she would take on that determined look that I knew so well, pull away, and continue to work.

One November day, as I watched her work with her imaginary yarn, I decided to go to Mother, instead of trying to pull her back to me. I admired her afghan and the pretty colors. She smiled! She had heard me.

I asked her whom the afghan was for, and in broken speech

she said, "My girl."

"It's beautiful!" I told her, and it really was. The love and dedication from my frail mother, to finish this gift of love, was a beautiful thing!

"I'll make sure she gets it." I smiled at her and began to sing her song.

"Twilight is stealing over the sea."

An amazing thing happened. My mother stopped her crocheting, and she began to sing. She only hit every other word or so, but oh, those words were precious to me. As I started to sing the chorus, I became aware of a bird singing outside the window. I walked to the window as I sang, and there, perched on the cement ledge of the fourth-floor window, was a red and brown finch, singing his heart out! What a sight we were that day, the little bird, my mother, and I, singing at the top of our lungs!

One month later, I was listening to the tape at my mother's funeral. My mind flashed back to that moment in time with my mother singing along. I closed my eyes, and I could hear my mother's clear soprano voice. A sweet peace enveloped me, bringing comfort to my heart.

I will always believe that God sent that song to us. As for the little bird . . . well, he must have been an angel, sent to put a song in our hearts at a time when we needed it most.

39

POWERFUL SURPRISE

MARY BETH OOSTENBRUG

"Your loved one will be placed on our waiting list" is what I usually have to say to families. *Oh, I hate having to tell them that. How I wish we could serve them all,* I frequently thought. Often, I give tours of our homes to prospective residents and their families, and I explain our waiting list, which currently has eighteen names on it. We own three homes, each full to their capacity, and we could easily fill three more. Openings rarely occur. But when they do, admitting a new resident is a joyful responsibility of mine.

I'm the executive director for a Christian organization that serves adults with intellectual disabilities. I begin most days by asking God to guide my words, attitude, and actions, so that His love is shown to all I encounter, particularly my staff. A few months ago, unsuspecting, I was led down a path that would reveal God's grace in a powerful and surprising way. A sad situation was the catalyst for this surprise.

"Some days I feel like I can't do this anymore, or that I really don't know what I'm doing," Lisa said, with her voice quivering.

"Lisa, I rely on your expertise in working with our residents. You have a great understanding of Brad's aggressive behaviors and how to respond to them. I really appreciate your talents, and you help me make tough decisions," I confided.

Tears came to her eyes. "Oh, that makes me feel so much better. I count on your strength to help me when I'm feeling lost."

Lisa is the supervisor in one of our homes where Brad lived with his four housemates. We serve them by providing daily living skill development and twenty-four-hour supervision. In the weeks following my meeting with Lisa, Brad's behaviors became much worse. It wasn't working out for him to live with us. It saddened me greatly, as I had to make the tough decision to let him go. But where? Brad's family needed to have him live near them.

"I'll make sure he's happy and well cared for, wherever he's served," I reassured Lisa. Inside, I hurt for Brad, for his family, and for my staff. We all work hard, but sometimes we just can't untangle every snag. When that happens, I try my best to console staff and remind myself to trust God. After someone is discharged, we all feel a spiritual loss. It's also my job to consider the financial loss. I need to fill vacancies as quickly as possible. I pray about it, never knowing how God will answer.

About a month before the discharge decision, I was giving a tour of one of our homes to the Millers, an elderly couple. Their son, Danny, who has disabilities, lived in a facility thirty miles away. They had faithfully traveled there to visit him, twice a month, for fifty-two years. Finally, it had become too challenging for them to make the trip, so they agreed to look into local facilities. As we walked through the house, Ben and Helen exclaimed, "This is a lovely home, and it's so close to where we live. It would be a dream come true if Danny could live here!"

They were both quite sweet and such fun, as they shared stories of growing up eighty years earlier, on this very street. Sadly, I thought, *It'll never work out to serve their son, until after they're gone. We have no openings and there's that waiting list. Oh! This is one of those days when I have to let people hope when there is none. I don't like this part of my job.* "God, give me strength."

I added Danny's name to our list. With each name added, the burden became greater. *I want to show God's love to all these people and relieve their families of some of the care and worry. We need to build more houses and serve as many as we can. We're just not able to do it fast enough,* I worried.

Our plan was to build a fourth home and serve five persons from our waiting list. We also needed to replace our old and too-small house with one that was handicap-accessible and would let us serve a fifth person in it. Both were future goals, unfortunately, and wouldn't relieve my burden anytime soon.

In the ensuing weeks, I tried to solve the issue of Brad's discharge. A facility that could serve Brad was only thirty miles away, but it, too, had no openings. They said, "We are completely full, so the only way we could admit Brad would be if you'd consider serving someone currently living here, in exchange."

Hmm, exchange one person for another. Brad would be happy there, and we'd serve someone else here. Would that work? Lisa and I scheduled a visit for the next day. When we were ushered into the activity room and introduced to the client, it turned out to be Danny! We met with him and talked with his staff. Our admissions committee met, and we decided he'd be a great fit for the vacancy. Danny's parents were ecstatic, and I was secretly smirking at God's hand in this turn of events. *Well, God, I hadn't seen* that *one coming! We're serving Danny now, after all!* But God wasn't done yet.

After Danny's first month with us, I talked about our organization's future plans to build another home next to Danny's, with his dad, Ben. I explained how the two homes would share a large, common yard, a patio, and it would be fenced in, for safety. "All the residents will have the ability to go outside on their own," I explained. He smiled and I saw the hint of a tear in his eye.

About two weeks later, I visited Ben and Helen to touch base with them about Danny's move and adjustment. I didn't even have a chance to ask, "How do you think Danny is adjusting?"

Ben immediately inquired, "How much do you need to build that new house?"

"Our Capital Campaign took place two years ago, so we have another year to gather pledge money. When we have enough, we'll build." Then I shared the dollar amount still needed.

"We're going to give you the entire amount you need to

get that home built right away. We want to see it built before we're gone!" he proclaimed.

Good thing I hadn't taken a drink of my lemonade. I would have choked. "Oh my, you two. That's an amazing gift! You're extremely generous to do this!"

"Well, we just love how Danny has adjusted, and we love your organization. We want to see him enjoy that yard now, while we still can. And this way, you can use your Capital Campaign money to replace your old house next year."

God must have been laughing hard, seeing my astonishment. On my way home, I remembered three months back when I met the Millers and how sad I'd been, assuming we'd not be able to serve Danny for a long time.

I'm so grateful for getting to serve Danny because we're not just serving him; we're giving his parents assurance and peace of mind about Danny's welfare. In addition, I thank God that we get to serve five more people and their families this year. And another new person next year!

We're breaking ground for the new home next week. I'm eager to fill it with people who need us. I'm excited thinking about the residents going outside, into the yard, whenever they wish. And I'm still in awe at how God answered so many prayers, in such amazing ways. God's grace was, indeed, a powerful surprise.

40

WHEN GOD SAID NO

MARTY PRUDHOMME

One bright spring day, my husband, Bill, came home announcing the end of my safe little world. He wanted me to leave everything that was familiar and move to another town thirty-five miles away. That might not seem far to some people, but to me it was a lifetime away. It meant leaving our church, our friends, the children's schools, and the house I loved. I did not want a new house.

This would also mean relocating my elderly mom who lived with us. Mom could not be left alone, so this move also meant replacing the wonderful Christian ladies who helped care for her. I would have to start all over again trying to find trustworthy nurse's aides. I'd heard such horror stories about bringing in help for the elderly that I was very concerned. God had been so good to us, but would He do it again in another place? I was comfortable with these ladies, and Mom liked them. This move would not be easy for her, either.

I tried my best to talk Bill out of moving. Our twenty-year-old son, Michael, would probably be leaving home in the next few years and our daughter, Rebecca, would be a junior in high school in the fall. It seemed foolish to disrupt her at such a crucial time in her life. I did not want to pull her away from her lifelong friends. I felt this move could wait until Rebecca finished high school. She would be going away to college in two years. Why build a big house for all of us when our family would soon be shrinking? I thought I was making a reasonable request.

But Bill was determined to move; there was no reasoning with him. Since he was a child he had loved the community of Mandeville across Lake Pontchatrain from New Orleans. He remembered the lovely trees and resort community atmosphere and was unwavering in his resolve to leave the city.

I would go out on our patio night after night and cry, "God, help me. I need Your grace to do this thing." I felt like my whole life was slipping away. I had lifelong friends in the community where we lived, and our children had grown up with our neighbors' children. We had been saved in the church down the road. That community was near and dear to my heart.

I asked all my friends to pray for me. I did not want to move, but I did not want to resent my husband, either. I could not understand why Bill wanted to move now. He was six years away from early retirement, and our move would mean a commute of thirty-five miles in heavy traffic, twice every day. I could not see any advantages in moving at this time in our lives. Why not wait until he retired?

I knew God could deal with my husband if he was making a mistake, but what about me? I tried to reason with God: "Lord, if this move is a big mistake, I am going to be in the middle of Bill's blunder." I cried many tears, but I still could not find peace in the middle of this "storm."

One evening while commiserating out on the back patio, I heard a small, still voice. It was not a physical voice, but it came from deep inside: "Go, and don't complain." I was sure I had imagined hearing this. The next night, as I was praying, the Lord whispered, "Go. I will take care of you."

This was not what I wanted to hear, but night after night, out on the patio, God continued to whisper, "Go." He let me know that His grace was sufficient for me. On my own, I would never make it, at least not without a whole lot of grumbling, anger, and resentment.

The long process of putting our house up for sale began. We had to sell before we could afford to move into another house. Because the real estate market was extremely depressed, our realtor told us the average time to sell a house in our neighborhood was two years. I thought, *Well, Lord, it's in Your hands.* Our house sold in three months—just in time to get Rebecca into Mandeville High School for her junior year.

To make things worse, Bill wanted to build a house instead of buying an existing one. I dreaded the process. I knew it would take a year of my life for something that did not have any eternal value. Bill would be working, so I would be left to deal with the contractor and subcontractors. Building a custom house is a major ordeal with lots of pitfalls.

Everything but the bare essentials went into storage while we looked for property. Meanwhile we all crammed into a small apartment, putting Mom in the downstairs bedroom. The rest of us moved into the two tiny bedrooms upstairs.

There were no four-bedroom apartments in the area, so Rebecca and Michael were forced to share a room. What a mess that was. After a week Michael dragged his mattress into the tiny attic with the water heater in order to get away from his teenage sister.

My prayers changed. I cried, "We are building this house for five people, and in a few years three of them will be gone. Mom is not well, and I know our time with her is short. Lord, please fill up this house for Your glory. I don't want to live in a big, empty house."

The first week we moved into the apartment I met a Christian lady named Beverly who sat with the elderly. She came to work for us and recommended other ladies who were wonderful with my mom. The Lord had outdone Himself. The ladies not only helped me take care of Mom, but they became my personal friends. Why did I ever worry?

However, building the house was a totally different story. Everything that could go wrong, did. I went to the property daily, working with the subcontractors in order to correct their mistakes. Our main contractor was building five houses at the same time and was not looking after our house the way he should. Many mistakes were made because of his neglect. The carpenters even put the chimney straight through the middle of the upstairs closet. The bathroom shower was installed in the wrong place, and the sink in the laundry was not properly connected and flooded the downstairs. There were many other things that went wrong. Fortunately they all were corrected before we moved in. It was one of the most frustrating and stressful years of my life.

Yet in the midst of the constant pressure, I knew God was with me. He gave me joy and wisdom to solve each problem one by one. God had a plan in spite of all the chaos.

Our builder began to talk to me about the nerve-racking overload he felt building five houses at once. Two of his clients were suing him. He asked how I could be so calm in light of all the mess-ups. This inquiry gave me the opportunity to let him know I was praying for him, and God opened the door for me to share the gospel with him. Eventually our builder gave his life to the Lord. He knew many people in the community and became a wonderful witness for God. After he finished our house, he decided to take an entire year off work in order to spend time with his family and seek the Lord's direction for his life.

By the time we moved into our new home, it was evident God was working in my husband's life. Before we moved, he was a nominal Christian, only going to church out of obligation on Sundays. God stirred his heart to become involved in our new church. Bill began helping out with projects around the church. Then he taught a Bible study and finally was asked to join the church's Deacon Board. God was definitely working. I began to wonder if this was why we moved.

The first year we lived in Mandeville, my mom passed away. Our son, Michael, joined the National Guard and was deployed to Kuwait. Our daughter, Rebecca, went away to college. As the house emptied out, the Lord began to answer my prayers to fill it up. Lee Anne, our church choir director's daughter, came to live with us her last year in high school. Her dad's job had transferred her family to Florida. Lee Anne was quite involved in her school and didn't want to leave all her friends in her senior year. After Lee Anne graduated, she moved back with her parents to attend college.

No sooner had Lee Anne moved out when we received a phone call from a stranger saying they heard we took in people who had needs. Susan was a battered wife with three young children. She and her kids lived with us for several months. We prayed fervently for her husband during that time.

After a few months, I met her husband and God prompted me to ask him if he had been abused as a child. He admitted his father had abused him. This one question brought about a series of events that began Susan's husband's healing and the restoration of his family. Once again God had outdone Himself answering our prayers.

Michael came home from Kuwait and married his sweetheart, so our house was empty again. However, that soon changed when Katie came to live with us. We met her at church and soon became close friends. She was a Pied Piper to all the young girls at church—her laughter was contagious.

Katie was a college student living in very difficult circumstances. At first she would come to the house on weekends to have a quiet place to study; eventually she came to stay. The Lord did many miracles in Katie's life during the time she lived with us, and we called her our adopted daughter. Katie stayed almost three years until she graduated from college and left for the mission field in the Philippines. After several years she came back to the States to become the associate pastor of a church. Katie now lives in Texas with her two adopted sons.

Our daughter, Rebecca, came home long enough to get married and move out again. Before long, our new pastor, his wife, and four boys needed a place to stay on weekends. They came from a town fifty miles away and stayed in our home while trying to sell their house. Like us, they could not afford two residences at once, so our almost-empty house was the perfect place for them to stay. It took a year to sell their house and buy one near our church. It was a great year, and we were blessed to have them stay with us.

Right now, we have a gentleman staying with us for a few months until he can find a job and move into a place of his own.

When I think about all the Lord has done in our lives and the lives of the people who have lived with us, I am in awe. I will forever be grateful that God knew what was best and did not answer my initial prayers about the move. His grace not only sustained me through this time but gave me great joy in the journey. I asked the Lord to change Bill's mind; instead He changed many lives, including mine. God's plans were best after all.

41

WALLET WOES

EMMARIE LEHNICK

On a brisk December Saturday in 1957, my husband, Eddie, and I decided to drive the seventy-five miles from our small town to Amarillo to finish our Christmas shopping. This would be the first long trip for our three-month-old baby girl, Debbie.

Being frugal with Eddie's teacher salary, we managed to just make ends meet from month to month. We had saved twenty-five dollars to buy the remaining gifts. I had made potholders, aprons, clove/orange fragrance balls, and cup towels for the women on our list. We still needed to buy a couple's gift, a man's gift, and something special for Debbie.

Car seats at that time were a thing of the future. We had a rocking carrier to use in the house and car, but it did not have straps to keep the baby safe. Generally as the passenger, I held the baby, whom I cocooned in several pink blankets because as a new mother I imagined a baby needed extra warmth.

When we reached Polk Street, we searched for a place close to Woolworth's. Cars filled all the parallel parking spaces. Eddie circled the block and handed me two ten-dollar bills. I reached for my purse and quickly put the money in my billfold. He pulled alongside a parked car, and I gathered Debbie in my arms, grabbed my purse, and opened the door.

"I'll try to find a parking place and join you," Eddie said. "If I can't find one, I'll drive around and watch for you."

The impatient man in the car behind us angrily honked his horn. Slamming the door shut, I hurried to the curb and into Woolworth's.

Wrestling my blanketed baby in my left arm and selecting gifts with my right, I found several items to purchase. With loaded arms, I waited for the clerk to finish with one buyer and help me. When the clerk nodded to me, I placed my items on the counter. As I shopped, I had mentally calculated the needed amount. The clerk totaled my bill, and it was the same as I had figured. I reached into my purse for my billfold. It was not there. I laid Debbie on the counter so that I could investigate every inch of my purse. The billfold was not there. My hands shook as I emptied the contents of my purse onto the counter. Panic seized me.

"I can't find my billfold," I said to the saleslady. "I had it in the car and put my money in it." My trembling voice showed my alarm.

The line of people waiting behind me had grown. They seemed sympathetic yet eager to check out.

"I'll hold these things awhile, and you can come back," said the accommodating cashier.

Stuffing everything back in my purse, I clasped Debbie to me. My entire being quivered, and anguished tears flooded my eyes as I retraced the aisles I had used. My eyes frantically scanned the floor and counters and swept over every inch where I had shopped. I prayed silently, "Please help me, Lord."

Some people stared at my near hysterical state and whispered to each other.

Thoughts rushed through my head. "What would Eddie think? My stupidity had cost us our Christmas money. Why had I been so careless? That driver's impatience caused me to hurry to get out of the car. I can't blame anyone but myself. Eddie had kept five dollars for lunch and gas. He will wish he had never married me. Oh Father, help me."

I stumbled to the front door like a beaten servant whose bleeding lacerations from a lashing whip left her unbalanced and confused. Hugging my bundled baby to me, I sobbed into the soft folds of her blanket.

Eddie spotted me and stopped alongside a parked car. He leaned over to open the passenger door as I scrambled in. "Didn't you find anything?" he asked, noting that I had no packages.

I burst into tears, trying to talk while weeping uncontrollably. "I lost my billfold. When I started to pay the clerk, I couldn't find it. I went back and looked everywhere that I had been in the store. I searched and searched. It was not there. I lost our money. I don't know what we will do. Santa can't leave Debbie anything. I am just plain stupid. I won't blame you if you scream at me. I'm so sorry."

"I'll find a parking place, and we'll go back and look in the street and in the store," he said with a sympathetic, controlled voice.

"We won't find it."

"Well, it's worth a try. Don't give up. Everything will be okay."

After parking a block from Woolworth's, we walked back and searched the curb, the street, the sidewalk, and the aisles of the store. All to no avail.

The words beat in my aching head. "The billfold is gone. Please help us, Lord."

Dejectedly, we walked back to the car. "I'll go to the police station and see if someone turned it in," Eddie said.

"There is no way in this world someone would turn in a billfold with twenty dollars in it."

Eddie drove to the police station and strode inside while Debbie and I waited in the car. I prayed that they had my billfold, but I felt my prayer was useless.

When Eddie returned, he slid behind the wheel, looked at me, and related the events in the station. "I told the policeman at the desk about your getting out of the car and going into Woolworth's and that you couldn't find your billfold to pay for your purchases. He asked me to describe it. I said it was brown and had two ten-dollar bills in it. The policeman looked in the lost-and-found drawer and opened a brown billfold.

"He asked if I had any identification. I took out my wallet to show him my driver's license. Then he said, 'Oh, never mind. There are several pictures of you in this billfold.'

"I guess I looked utterly relieved. He said that a homeless man found it in the gutter in front of Woolworth's. The vagrant man told the policeman that he looked inside the billfold and saw the money. Then, something inside him made him bring it to the station immediately before he had second thoughts.

"The officer said that the man did not want to leave his name or get a reward because he felt rewarded enough by just doing the right thing. Then, the policeman told how the man smiled broadly and walked out with shoulders a bit straighter."

Eddie grinned and handed me the orphaned billfold.

"I can't believe it. He walked all the way to the police station to turn in a billfold containing money. Praise God! How could I ever have doubted my prayer? Homeless Man, wherever you are, may God bless you."

Eddie smiled and said, "I think He already has."

42

A LETTER FROM DADDY

JULIA M. TOTO

My God shall supply all your need according to
His riches in glory by Christ Jesus.
PHILIPPIANS 4:19 NKJV

Daddy had big plans. He was a visionary and a stickler for detail. The only thing was, Daddy hadn't planned to die when he did.

For sixty-four years, Mama had been the wind beneath Daddy's wings and had learned to make a home anywhere his dreams took them. It was evidence of a great marriage, I always said, and a life together well lived. When he died, however, Mama was left to decide which dreams to live and which ones to let rest in peace with Daddy.

Grandma always said we were part gypsy, and I suspect it's true because my parents made their home not in one place but in three, all of them modest and for the most part built by the sweat of their brow. Daddy loved them all. But when he died, Mama had three closets to go through, three garages to empty, and three toothbrushes to discard. She faced the daunting task of selling the family homestead back East, finishing their winter house out West, and making repairs on their cabin in the foothills of the Ozark Mountains.

She also had to decide what to do with a special piece of land they'd purchased there nearly thirty-five years ago, and on which Daddy had decided they'd settle down . . . someday. Unspoiled and canopied by hardwood, its gentle slope bordered a gravel road that meandered through the woods, beside a horse pasture, and ended at the pristine waters of the Illinois River.

Three decades and four generations of memories romped through those piney woods. Picnics with children, grandchildren, and great-grandchildren. Bird watching, flower picking. Dreaming, planning, measuring, and shooting elevations.

You see, some men golf for recreation. Daddy drew house plans. Then he'd build them and move Mama into them, and sometimes he'd even finish them.

For this particular piece of lot, he'd designed one last beauty of a house whose blueprints grew exponentially as it became Daddy's hobby in his later years. He'd thought of everything—the direction of the sunrise, an oversized deck, a bunkroom for the grandkids, and quarters for a caretaker should he or Mom ever need one. This was to be the home in which they'd enjoy their sunset years. His latest addition had been an in-ground swimming pool and bathhouse, no doubt drawn one sultry summer day.

Over time, weeds grew, Black Jack branches littered the ground, and a carpet of dead leaves heaped high as my knees. When it became apparent that none of our family would ever build there, Mama resolved it was time to put the lot up for sale. So, four years after Daddy died, a For Sale by Owner sign stood where his dream house might have been, and I played the role of realtor.

"Yes, ma'am. We'd be happy to show you the property this weekend," I said to the interested buyer on the other end of the phone. "I'll gather all the information you've asked for and call you in the morning."

I tossed the phone on my desk and hung my head. Where would I find the information she was asking for? I had a good idea where the lot line was; after all, I'd walked it enough times with Daddy. But many years had passed since then, and the steel property pins were buried deep beneath years of ice storm and tornado damage.

Earlier in the week my husband, Lou, had requested a copy of the plat from the county clerk's office, but when it came to us, the dimensions were illegible. Armed with bug spray and knee-high boots, we'd combed the forest floor with our trusty flea market metal detector, but that had proven futile as well.

Clutching a magnifying glass, I studied the plat again. "Is that a three?"

"I think it's an eight." Lou squinted as he leaned over the fuzzy numbers. "Nope. Nope. Maybe a nine. Or a six."

I sighed and shuffled again through the folder that Mama had given us. "Maybe we've missed something in here."

"Nothing. I've looked."

We craned our necks over a faded copy of a map. A

greenbelt sloped to the south of the property, but where in the world would we ever find information on the lot directly behind? Who owned it? How big was it? Did anyone have plans to build next door? I couldn't say, but the potential buyer wanted to know.

I tossed the file aside, feeling discouraged. Why hadn't I been better prepared to sell? Oh, me of little faith. I closed my eyes and whined more than prayed, asking God for wisdom, favor, and for His will to be done.

Later that night after dinner at Mama's, I rolled up the blueprints, snapped the rubber band around the bundle, and handed it to her. "Thanks, Mama. Nothing here that really helps, though. If only we could locate those property pins before showing the lot this weekend."

"Sorry I can't be of more help, honey. Your daddy took care of all of this stuff. I just listened to his plans, nodded, and signed where he told me to sign."

I smiled. Such trust. "I've gone through everything you've given me. Lots of notes, old deeds, magazine clips with landscape ideas. Did you know Daddy was planning a Japanese water garden?"

"Oh, the wildlife would have loved that." Mama chuckled. "I'll go look again in the file cabinet. Maybe I missed something."

I appreciated the effort but wasn't optimistic. Mama was trying so hard to help us help her. Daddy had been the same way. I didn't mind doing the legwork for them; I only hoped it wasn't all in vain.

She returned with another file folder and handed it to me. "Don't know where this one was hiding, but let's see if it has anything in it that will help."

I opened the tattered folder, and my breath caught in my chest. Lying on top was a detailed sketch of their lot and the one directly behind it. The dimensions on each side were clearly printed, as well as the required setback. All the property pins were circled in red and notated by precise measurements. With it was a letter in Daddy's handwriting, dated ten years before he died. He'd never mailed it. The letter was addressed to my husband and me.

> *Dear Julia and Lou,*
> *Here's the sketch of the lot on the ridge and the one behind it. Note that the road has a gentler bend than is shown, so the steel pin at the property line between the two properties is actually back in the woods a ways.*
>
> *I think the northern portion of that lot drops off pretty steep, so it probably is not a good lot for building on. But anyway, I believe this sketch is reasonably close to the actual shape and dimension of the lot behind us. Other than the weather being a little cool—but sunny—everything else is about the same as usual.*
>
> *Love ya,*
> *Dad*

By the time I finished reading, hot tears burned and I could hardly speak. God had heard my meager prayer and had answered it. This wasn't the first time I'd been able to help Mama by finding information Daddy had written down in a file or a notebook somewhere. But it was the first time the information ever had my name on it. It was like getting one more hug from him.

I ran my fingers over Daddy's familiar southpaw scroll then smoothed the corners of the letter and tucked it, along with the map, back into the folder. This was what we needed to sell their lot. Mama could sleep well tonight.

Thanks, Daddy. I love you, too.

WRITER BIOS

Former special education teacher and social worker, **Mary Dodge Allen** has been married thirty-seven years to the love of her life, and together they have one adult son. Her nonfiction articles have been published in regional newspapers. One of her short love stories was included in the anthology *My Love to You Always*, published by OakTara in October 2012. She is currently working on an inspirational WWII novel set in Florida. Connect with her at www.MaryDodgeAllen.com.

Marlene Anderson is an inspirational and motivational speaker and author. She has a master's degree in psychology/counseling, is a licensed counselor, and is a member of Northwest Christian Writers Association. She published her first book, *A Love So Great, A Grief So Deep*, after the death of her husband, and she continues to share her passion for God along with her training and life experiences through her speaking, blogs, and online monthly newsletters. For additional information and publications, go to her website, www.focuswithmarlene.com. God took her beloved son to be with Him four years ago.

From a lifetime of experience in film and video production, **Max Elliot Anderson** brings visual excitement and heart-pounding action to his adventures and mysteries for middle-grade readers. Ten books are published, and ten more are contracted. Visit his blog at http://booksandboys.blogspot.com.

Toni M. Babcock is a Christian writer and author of *The Stone Writer: Christian Fiction for Young Readers and Teens*. She also contributes her short articles and devotions on a regular basis to www.knittedtogetherbygod.com and www.faithtruthandlovemag.com. Toni is a member of Faith Writers, and her profile page can be viewed at www.faithwriters.com.

Sheldon K. Bass is a Christian minister, writer, inspirational speaker, and Bible teacher, who has a passion for people of all cultures and a heart for proclaiming the gospel of Jesus Christ. Since November 2012, dozens of his articles and devotions have been published in books, magazines, and across the web, bringing hope and encouragement while pointing to God's amazing grace. Sheldon is widely traveled, currently lives in Indianapolis,

Indiana, and is working on a novel and a devotional book geared toward healing past hurts. He blogs on maturing in faith at growingupinjesus. com.

Dr. James Braley holds a B.A. in Christian education and an M.A. in curriculum and supervision. An LL. D. was awarded by Biola University for his work with Christian schools. Besides teaching at every grade level—elementary through graduate school—he has taught extensively at conferences and conventions across the United States and in eleven other countries. Publications include articles in national magazines and chapters in books helpful to Christian schools. He served as a consultant with publishing companies, and developed the Character Foundation Curriculum now used in many schools. Dr. Braley and his wife, Faye, live in Cottonwood, Arizona.

Lorraine M. Castle's passion is writing. She is living her dream of writing and assisting writers in reaching their goals as a Virtual Author's Assistant. She shares her passion as she assists authors with their books. Lorraine's website is www.castlevirtualsolutions.com, where you can read her blog and learn more about her. Born and raised in Philadelphia, Pennsylvania, Lorraine now resides in South Jersey. She can be found on Facebook at https://www.facebook.com/CastleVirtualSolutions?ref=hl.

Carol Chase is a retired administrative supervisor who lives in British Columbia. She enjoys gardening and reading and has a deep passion for prayer. She and her husband spent many years circumnavigating the world in a small sailboat.

Shirley Corder is a registered nurse, cancer survivor, and internationally published author. She lives near the ocean in Port Elizabeth, South Africa, with her husband, Rob. Her book, *Strength Renewed: Meditations for Your Journey Through Breast Cancer*, is published by Revell/Baker, and she has contributed to ten anthologies to date. For relaxation, Shirley enjoys making music, photography, and walking on the beach. Please visit Shirley's cyber home at www.shirleycorder.com.

Beau Cornerstone lives in Western Australia. She is married with three children and writes whenever she can snatch time for herself. Beau has homeschooled for the past twenty years and produces educational puzzles for teachers and homeschoolers. Links to her free e-resources for home-schooling families can be found on her occasional blog: http://beaucorner-stone.blogspot.com.au/. She also has a passion for inspiring young adults to rebel against society's low expectations. Her fiction encourages Christian young adults to develop a creation worldview, abstain until marriage, and be godly examples to their peers. Visit http://beaucornerstone.blogspot.com.au/2012/06/rebelutionaries-series.html.

Linda Veath Cox, a retired secretary, loves to read. But occasionally she tries her hand at writing. Her works have been published in *All My Bad Habits I Learned from Grandpa* (Thomas Nelson), *The One-Year Life Verse Devotional* (Tyndale), *Life Lessons from Grandparents* (Write Integrity), *Love Is a Verb* (Bethany House), *Chicken Soup for the Soul's I Can't Believe My Dog Did That*, and *God Still Meets Needs* (Mark Littleton). Linda is a regular contributor to DivineDetour.com and lives in a small town in the Midwest with the "Bone Mafia," her two indoor/outdoor mutts.

Tracy Crump's articles, devotionals, and short stories have appeared in publications such as *Focus on the Family*, *Light & Life*, *Parent Life*, and *Mature Living*. Chicken Soup for the Soul had published a dozen of her stories, and she conducts workshops and webinars on writing for Chicken Soup through Write Life Workshops, which she co-directs. Tracy is a columnist for *Southern Writers Magazine*, manages an online critique group, and edits *The Write Life* newsletter. She also enjoys teaching at writers conferences. But if you really want to make Tracy smile, ask her about Nellie. Visit Tracy at www.WriteLifeWorkshops.com or www.TracyCrump.com.

Jeri Darby is a writer and has worked as an RN for over thirty years. She is active in women's ministry.

Kimberly Davidson is a board-certified biblical counselor and spiritual development coach, helping women mend their souls. She received her M.A. in specialized ministry from Western Seminary, and her B.A. in health sciences and nutrition from the University of Iowa. Kimberly has ministered to women for over ten years, from within prison walls to youth centers, inspiring others to empower God to meet their emotional and spiritual needs. She is the founder of Olive Branch Outreach, a ministry dedicated to bringing hope and restoration to those struggling with body image, abuse, and food addiction. Kimberly is the author of five books. Connect with Kimberly either through her website at olivebranchoutreach.com or on Facebook.

Bonnie Mae Evans is a registered nurse and writer. She has completed her first Christian novel for which she is currently seeking representation. She is a member of Mountain Christian Writer's Group, as well as Lancaster Christian Writers. Her devotionals have been published in several books, including *God Stories 7*, *God Stories 8*, *Blessed Are You*, and *A Daily Walk with God*, published in Kenya for WGM missionaries to share with new converts. Serving the Lord and sharing His great love through stories is the true joy of her heart. You can follow her on Twitter: @BonnieMaeEvans.

Nancy B. Gibbs is a pastor's wife, mother, and grandmother. She is the author of ten books and has been published in numerous magazines, anthologies, devotional guides, and newspapers. She is also a motivational speaker and shares God's Word naturally. Visit her at www.nancybgibbs.com.

Kristi Huseby is the women's ministry director at a rapidly growing church community in West Michigan. She has a tremendous love for the many women she mentors and believes in the power of God's Word to change lives. Kristi and her husband, Harold, have been married for twenty-eight years. They live in Grand Rapids, Michigan. They have four boys and have recently added an exchange son from South Korea to the mix. She loves grabbing a cup of coffee with a friend, reading a good book, watching her boys turn into men, and seeing God transform a life. Connect with her at www.brokenandredeemed-kristi.blogspot.com.

Kathleen Kohler writes stories of hope rooted in her own life experiences for magazines and anthologies. She and her husband of thirty-five years live in the Pacific Northwest, and have three children and seven grandchildren. Kathleen enjoys gardening, travel, and watercolor painting, and is always amazed how God intervenes in our lives. Visit www.kathleenkohler.com to read more of her published work, including stories that have appeared in several Chicken Soup for the Soul books. And don't forget to visit her life notes page to enter her latest drawing.

Emmarie Lehnick of Amarillo, Texas, is a retired English/speech teacher with B.S. and M.A. degrees. She has written stories that have been included in several *Cup of Comfort* and *Rocking Chair Reader* anthologies, as well as other publications. She and her husband, Edward, have a daughter, Debbie, a son, Mark, and four grandboys.

Bonnie Leon is the author of nineteen novels, including the popular Alaskan Skies series. Bonnie and her husband live in Southern Oregon. They have three children and seven grandchildren.

Deedre Martz lives in Louisville, Colorado. She is a small business manager, writer, editor, animal caregiver, and avid gardener.

Jade Mazarin is a board-certified Christian counselor in private practice. She holds an MA in marriage and family therapy and a BA in religion. Jade enjoys sharing her personal experiences in order to bring guidance and hope. Along with counseling, Jade has always loved to write. She writes articles on spiritual and emotional health, and authored the book *The Heart's Journey to Freedom*. She also creates college curriculum for the company Education Portal. Jade lives in Vero Beach, Florida, and offers out-of-state counseling via Skype. Her website is www.jademazarin.net.

Loretta Miller Mehl writes stories about her life as a sharecropper's child. She has many published stories, devotionals, and articles. She is blessed with four children, thirteen grandchildren, and two great-grandchildren. A former resident of Southern California for forty years, she spent several years as a secretary for the City of San Marino and earlier years as a telegraph operator for Western Union.

Jen Miller is the author of her true "hell to healing" life story, *Now I Lay Me Down to Sleep: The Story of Sara*. She is a multi-published writer, professional book editor, and a senior chaplain-minister dedicated to women. She is the founder of The Sara Ministry (www.sara-ministry.com) and national Moms of Marines Support (M.O.M.S. www.moms-of-marines-support.com). Her work also includes praise and worship music under contract with CCLI for public use. Jen is available for small group forums for writers and for women's small groups focusing on biblical spiritual growth in practical life. She'd love to hear from you at jen@sara-ministry.com.

Diane Nunley lives and writes in Hillsboro, Tennessee.

Mary Beth Oostenbrug has been published in *Facets* magazine, *Love Is a Verb*, *God Still Meets Needs*, and the *Upper Room*. As executive director of a faith-based agency that serves adults with intellectual disabilities, Mary Beth writes its quarterly newsletter. Mary Beth occasionally preaches and serves as a Stephen Leader for her local church. She is working on her memoir and a book about her work. She loves being a wife and grandmother, gardening, painting, and riding her bike. Mary Beth always tries to turn life's painful times into blessings, thus the name of her blog: http://makeroflemonade.wordpress.com.

Jane Owen, a retired teacher, wrote her first story when she was seven years old. "Sparky's Gone" told of her beloved dog's rescue. Writing as a gift for others continues to be Jane's passion. Her articles have appeared in the *Upper Room*, *In Touch* (online), and in publications by Guidepost Books, St. Martin's Press, and Bethany House. Jane and her husband live in a cabin in West Virginia, where the Lord keeps her focused on writing to bless others. Contact her at ladyjaneut@aol.com.

Melanie H. Platt writes as one of many expressions of communication. She works with her dogs, enjoys riding horses, and is intrigued by learning how to read and respond to animal body language. She is the author of several anthology stories and lives in Lafayette, Colorado.

Marty Prudhomme has written and taught Bible studies for twenty-five years. She is from Mandeville, Louisiana, and serves on the Louisiana State Leadership Team of Aglow International, a ministry of evangelism and prayer. Marty can be reached at HeavenlyDesignsbyMarty.com.

Suzette Pruit is a Houston, Texas, writer. She and her husband, Robert, have three children, three in-law children, and nine grandchildren. Suzette has worked as a newspaper reporter, editorial assistant, freelance writer, and La Leche League leader. She has served her churches in many capacities, mostly in adult Christian education. A lifelong Episcopalian and lover of Jesus, she is a member of Paler Memorial Episcopal Church. Suzette has published articles in both Christian and secular markets, and she has published the book *The Middle Ages: Navigating the Years from 40 to 60*.

Colleen L. Reece learned to read by kerosene lamplight in a home without running water or electricity . . . but filled with love for God and family. The "someday" book she dreamed of writing has been multiplied into *150 Books You Can Trust*, six million copies sold.

Tina Samples is a Colorado-based writer, speaker, and worship leader. Her new book, *Wounded Women of the Bible*, was just released in July 2013. She serves with her husband, David, at Grace River Church in Windsor, Colorado. Tina's publishing credits include *Guideposts*, *Extraordinary Answers to Prayer*, *Angels, Miracles, and Heavenly Encounters*, and *The One Year Life Verse Devotional*. She also contributed to *The Secret Place* devotional magazine, as well as *Quiet Hour* magazine. She takes joy in Jaren, Jillian, Zach, and baby Abigail. Contact her at www.tinasamples.com.

Donna Scales is a wife, mother, grandmother, mentor, Bible study leader, short-term missionary, and perennial volunteer. She has been a Cub Scout leader, Released-Time Program founder, teacher, and curriculum writer, and she has served on special needs school district and state level committees. Her latest role is that of skills trainer to Scott, who has lived on his own for thirteen years, caregiver to her ninety-five-year-old mother, and medical advocate/helper for her husband, who has pain and mobility issues. Oh yes, and she writes, too.

Sharon Sheppard is an award-winning freelancer who loves to write about ordinary people who have extraordinary experiences. She met heart transplant recipient Scott Stanley at the Mayo Clinic when her own husband was awaiting a stem cell transplant. Moved by Scott's courage and optimism, she hopes his story will inspire others. Sharon's four-hundred-plus articles have appeared in anthologies and literary journals, as well as such magazines as *Writer's Digest*, *Focus on the Family* magazine, the Sunday magazine of the *Minneapolis Star Tribune*, and dozens of others. She divides her time between Minnesota and the mountains of western Washington.

Shirley Shibley has been writing since childhood. She lives in Southern California near her three children and some of her thirteen grandchildren and six great-grandchildren. She is grateful to the Lord for all His gifts, especially salvation through the sacrifice of Jesus Christ. Check out her website for published writing at http://shirleyashibley.com.

Bobby Barbara Smith is well known for her inspirational short stories and poetry. Her works have been published in the Women of Faith anthology and also in several *Not Your Mother's Book* anthologies, along with many online publications. Bobby currently resides in the beautiful natural state of Arkansas, where she writes songs and performs with local bands and musicians. She loves animals and networks on Facebook to find homes for abused and neglected dogs. Bobby blogs at http://indy113.wordpress. com.

David Michael Smith writes from his hometown of Georgetown, Delaware, where he lives happily with his wife, Geri, daughter, Rebekah, and son, Matthew. He takes great joy in serving his Lord and Savior, Jesus, through a variety of earthly ministries, including inspirational writing. David is currently studying to be an ordained deacon in the North American Anglican Church. Contact David at davidandgeri@hotmail.com.

Patricia L. Stebelton is the author of romantic suspense mysteries *The Sleeping Matchbook*, *Watched*, and *Inherited Danger*, and short stories included in *Whispering in God's Ear*, *Angels, Miracles, and Heavenly*

Encounters 1, Falling in Love with You, as well as Guideposts Books. Patricia and her husband live in a picturesque town in the heart of Michigan. Patricia enjoys family activities, her writing, commissioned art projects, and camping. Contact her at plstebelton@yahoo.com.

Jack Taylor, PhD, has founded and cofounded nine organizations, has worked in Kenya for eighteen years, and currently pastors a congregation with representatives from over fifty nations. He lives in Vancouver, BC, Canada, with his wife, Gayle. His books include *One Last Wave* and *No Place to Run.*

Sue Tornai lives with her husband, John, and dog, Maggie, in Northern California. Many of her articles and stories have been published in Christian magazines and anthologies. When someone asks her what her most rewarding experience is, she says, "It's when I hear that something I wrote touched a heart or changed a life. That's why I write. I write to inspire people with God's amazing love."

Books were among **Julia Toto**'s best friends even before she could read, and she now writes to entertain and inspire others. Educator, published author, and ghostwriter, Julia's work appears in print and on the web. Her most rewarding role, however, is that of mother and grandmother. After residing in many places across the United States, Julia and her husband, the love of her life, now make their home in a stone cottage in the Ozark foothills.

Dawn Wilson, founder of Heart Choices Ministries, encourages women to glorify and enjoy God as they upgrade their lives through wise, biblical choices. She coauthored *LOL with God: Devotional Messages of Hope and Humor for Women* with Pam Farrel, and writes three blogs, including the encouraging UpgradeWithDawn.com. Dawn is also the San Diego chapter president for the Network of Evangelical Women in Ministry (NEWIM). She and her husband, Bob, have served together for four decades in churches and three national ministries. They have two married sons, three granddaughters, and a rascally maltipoo named Roscoe.